해석을 통한 **문해력** 기르기

문법을 배우고
단어를 외우고
해석을 하고, 문해력도 키우는
문장 해석 933

문법 문제 [440] 문항으로 문법에 자신감을 갖고

문장 속에 있는 [2,500]의 어휘를 가지고

문법별로 선정한 [933] 문장으로 해석에 문해력까지 완성!

문장을 해석하면서 문장 속에서 어휘가 의미하는 바를 이해하는 것이 어휘를 외우는 가장 좋은 방법입니다.

[42번째 교재 출간하는 고대 영문과 졸업한 28년 강의 경력의 저자]

책을 출간하면서

안녕하세요. 저자 안 천구입니다.

고려대학교 영문과를 졸업한 후 28년 동안 학생들에게 영어를 가르치면서, 학생들이 배운 문법을 활용해서 해석 할 수 있는 문장들이 있었으면 좋겠다는 생각이 들어 933 문장을 제작하게 되었으며 제가 출간 하게 되는 42번째 저서입니다. *[네이버 검색]*

933 문장에 나오는 문장들 50%는 제가 직접 제작한 문장들이고, 나머지는 다른 자료에서 찾아 참고하여 구성한 부분이 50%입니다. 덧붙여 대략 주요 문법에 따라 문법 문항수 440개 정도를 준비 하였습니다. 또한 학생들이 해석 하면서 외울 수 있도록 단어도 [2500]개를 난이도를 조절하여 구성하였으며, [단어 시험지 포함] 또한 제공합니다. 영어를 공부하는 학생들에게 많이 도움이 되기를 바랍니다.
감사합니다.

저자 안 천 구

[933 문장 해석의 특징]

문법을 배우고 나서 배운 문법을 활용하여 해석을 해 볼 수 있도록
각 문법별로 다양한 문제들로 구성하였습니다.
중2에서 고1정도의 난이도 기준으로
어휘도 English One에서 운영하는 네이버 카페에 준비하였습니다.
잉글리쉬 원 : 네이버 카페 (https://cafe.naver.com/egonenaver)에
가입한 후 해당 되는 단어들과 단어 시험도 볼 수 있습니다.

문법을 활용한 해석 연습

기본적인 문법 문제 제공

문장에 따른 단어 test 파일 제공

가르치는 선생님 혹은 각자 진도에 맞춰 해석

1년에 걸쳐 준비하였고, 문장 대부분은 자체 제작과 자료 활용으로 완성하였습니다.
해석하고, 독해실력을 두 단계 정도 올려 줄 수 있는 문장 933 입니다.

저자: **안 천 구** [An Glenn]
English One 어학원 원장 겸 강사

딱 한권으로 끝내는 구문 독해
Sure 중등 문법 I, II, III
The Better 문제만 있는 문법책 I, II
넥서스 중학영어 듣기 I, II, III

외 30권 이상의 저서가 현재 교보나 다른 서점에서 판매중입니다.

Contents...

Chapter 1 형식에 관한 문장
1-1. 1형식 .... 9 ~ 10
    Practice A
1-2. 2형식 .... 11 ~ 12
    Practice A
1-3. 3형식 .... 13 ~ 14
1-4. 4형식 .... 15 ~ 16
    Practice A
1-5. 5형식 .... 17 ~ 19
    Practice A

Chapter 2 조동사
2-1. can .... 21 ~ 22
2-2. may, might .... 23 ~ 24
2-3. must, have to, should .... 25 ~ 27
2-4. 나도 조동사 28

Chapter 3 비교급, 원급 그리고 최상급
3-1. 비교급 .... 30 ~ 31
3-2. 원급 비교 32
3-3. 최상급 33
    Stop 1 34

Chapter 4 시제
4-1. 현재 시제 .... 36 ~ 39
    Practice A
4-2. 현재완료 .... 40 ~ 43
    Practice A
4-3. 과거 완료 .... 44 ~ 45
    Practice A
    Stop 2 .... 46 ~ 47

Contents...

Chapter 5 to-부정사
5-1. 명사 자리에 나오는 경우   49 ~ 51
5-2. 형용사 역할을 하는   52 ~ 53
5-3. 부사 역할을 하는   54 ~ 57
       Practice A
5-4. 사역동사, 지각동사   58 ~ 62
       Practice A,B,C
5-5. too~to, 형용사+enough to   63 ~ 64

Chapter 6 동명사
6-1. 동명사   66 ~ 72
       Practice A,B

Chapter 7 수동태
7-1. 수동태   74 ~ 78
       Practice A,B
7-2. 조동사가 나오는 수동태   79 ~ 83
       Practice A,B,C
7-3. 5형식이 수동태 되면 2형식으로   84
7-4. by가 없거나 덩어리로 나오는 수동태   85 ~ 87
       Practice
       Stop 3   88 ~ 89

Chapter 8 분사
8-1. 명사를 앞에서 꾸며 주는 분사는 형용사   91 ~ 92
8-2. 지각동사   93
8-3. 형용사인 분사가 명사 뒤에 오는 경우   94 ~ 96
8-4. 감정을 나타내는 분사   97 ~ 99
       Practice A,B

Chapter 9 명사절, 형용사절

9-1. 명사절   101 ~ 105
      Practice A

9-2. 형용사절은 관계대명사 A 주격   106 ~ 110
      Practice A

9-2. 형용사절은 관계대명사 B 목적격   111 ~ 118
      Practice A,B

9-2. 형용사절은 관계대명사 C what   119 ~ 122
      Practice A

9-2. 형용사절은 관계대명사 D whose   123 ~ 124
      Practice A

Chapter 10 전치사

10-1. 전치사   126 ~ 131
      Practice A

Chapter 11 대명사

11-1. 부정대명사   133 ~ 134
11-2. 재귀대명사   135

Chapter 12 접속사

12-1. 양보   137 ~ 138
12-2. 상관   139 ~ 140

Chapter 13 가정법

13-1. 가정법 과거   142
13-2. 가정법 과거 완료   143 ~ 145
      Practice A, B

Chapter 1 형식에 관한 문장

1형식: 주어+동사만으로도 의미가 전달이 되는 문장

A bird **flew** to the north.
She **left** early this morning.

2형식: 주어의 상태나 신분을 나타내는 문장

This boy is not **my son**.
She got **upset**.

3형식: 목적어가 필요 해

I want **some water**.
He met **his uncle**.

4형식: 수여동사는 준다는 의미!

I gave **her** some money.
She bought **me** the guitar.

5형식: 목적어의 상태나 신분을 나타내는 문장

I found her **unhappy**.
He made me **a coach**.

1-1 1형식 [주어+동사만으로도 문장의 의미가 전달되는 형식]

> * She (S) + works (V) at a bank. (주로 문장 끝에 장소 혹은 시간을 나타내는 말이 나옴)
> * He gets up early.
> * 1형식 동사: come, arrive, appear, occur, be, exist, lie, stand, run, jump, go, disappear, leave

01 The sun **rises** in the east and sets in the west.

02 Good memories in childhood **last** long.

03 This medicine **works** well for a person like you.

04 There are **plenty of jobs** available in the area.

05 The flight is going to **depart** from Paris.

06 Temperatures **rise** above freezing in January.

07 Money was the only thing that **mattered** to him.

08 The papers **were lying** neatly on his desk.

09 Opportunities **exist** for students who make the effort.

10 The sun has **disappeared** behind a cloud.

11 Look, when I turn the key, nothing **happens**.

Practice A

▶ 다음 알맞은 형태를 고르시오.

01 She [lay, laid] on the floor, and took a deep breath.

02 The meeting will [last, be lasted] for 3 hours.

03 Something terrible [happened, was happened] here last night.

04 Mike will [rise, raise] his hand to ask more food.

05 They [arrived, were arrived] there early this morning.

06 Her child [was disappeared, disappeared] suddenly.

07 Turtles [lie, lay] their eggs at night.

08 Time [flies, is flown].

09 This restaurant [runs, is run] by his father.

10 Her mother [slept, was slept] all day yesterday.

11 She [lay, laid] the bag on the table.

12 The sun [rises, raises] in the east.

13 I don't believe ghosts [exist, are existed].

1-2 2형식 [동사 뒤에 명사나 형용사가 나와 주어의 신분이나 상태를 나타내는 형식]

* Mike is a **smart boy**. [주어의 신분]
* She looks **tired**. [형용사가 주어의 상태를 나타냄]

* 오감 동사 : feel, smell, taste, sound, look + 형용사
* 상태 동사 : become, go, get, turn, fall, run, come + 형용사 : ~이 되다.
* 지속 동사 : remain, stay, keep + 형용사: ~ (상태로) 있다.

01 We **are** all **worried** about air pollution.

02 The audience **looked bored** and started leaving the theater.

03 The sound **was growing** louder and louder.

04 These vegetables can **stay fresh** for a while.

05 Marriage and birthrates are not separate issues.

06 Free travel for children four years old and below are not available now.

07 Mike was polite to everyone because he didn't want to appear rude.

08 The value of the house sounds pretty high.

09 Young children often feel happier in a home environment.

10 His face turned red when he was asked a private question.

11 Eat right to stay heathy.

Practice A

❖ 괄호 안에 주어진 단어 중 알맞은 것을 고르시오.

01 She looks (happy / happily).

02 This food tastes. (good / well).

03 She moved (quick / quickly) to the door.

04 He read the book (quiet / quietly).

05 The oranges on the table smell (sweet / sweetly).

06 The apples in the basket taste (sour / sourly).

07 I felt (terrible / terribly) about the accident.

08 She can solve the problem. (easy / easily).

09 The question sounds (easy / easily).

10 This plan looks (simply / safe).

11 His sister sounds (friendly / sadly).

12 His little brother looks (lovely / nicely).

13 They tasted (delicious / deliciously).

14 She looked at him (angry / angrily).

15 His friends looked (wonderful / wonderfully).

1-3 3형식 [동사 다음에 목적어인 명사를 필요로 하는 문장 형식: ~을, 를]

* She (S) never eats (V) **fast food** (O).
* We didn't send **any gift** to him.
* Mike bought **a bracelet** for his mom.

01 I'm going to consider **your offer** carefully.

02 Children usually get **more individual attention** in small classes.

03 She raised **her hat** and took her seat.

04 He always makes excuses for being late.

05 He finally overcame his shyness in public.

06 Instead of fast food, I eat healthy food.

07 My father always encourages and supports me.

08 Protect yourself from harmful dust.

09 Make sure you get receipts for every item.

10 I'd like to share my room with my cousin.

11 We can't afford another overseas trip this year.

12 We don't have enough budget for a family trip.

13 The price includes everything except the stamps.

14 Before you start packing, lay out all the clothes on the bed.

15 After you reach a certain age, nobody wants to hire you.

16 Please, transfer the meat to warm plates.

17 Most hotels provide laundry service for their guests.

18 I recommended a reliable lawyer to my relative.

19 Mike left his baggage to us and went shopping

20 We are going to hold a concert to raise money for charity.

21 A leg injury may prevent David from playing in tomorrow's game.

1-4 4형식 [수여동사: ~에게 ~을 주다라고 해석되는 문장 형식]

* She sold **me** a valuable jewel. (4형식)
  팔았다 나에게 귀중한 보석을

* She sold **a valuable jewel** to me. (3형식)
  팔았다 귀중한 보석을 나에게

* He **left** his children small amount of money. [남겨주었다 그의 아이들에게]
* He **made** her a toy horse. [만들어 주었다 그녀에게]
* I **read** my daughter a bedtime story. [읽어 주었다 나의 딸에게]

01 She told **him a creative idea** and he accepted it.

02 He didn't send **me a gift** on my birthday and I became disappointed.

03 She didn't brought me the recipe for the onion soup, but I made it anyway.

04 Surprisingly, she lent me her total annual income.

05 He showed me much passion for music in his youth.

06 They tried to build their son a nice garden this year.

07 Both airlines offer travelers over 60 a discount.

08 His father managed to get him a job at the local factory.

09 It took her a lot of time to recover her health.

10 It cost me an arm and a leg to have my car repaired.

Practice A

❖ 다음 주어진 단어를 바르게 배열하시오.

01 (gave, some, me, money, she, to)
⇨ _____

02 (for, a flower, her, bought, I)
⇨ _____

03 (didn't, to, she, him, send, a letter)
⇨ _____

04 (her bag, showed, us, she, to)
⇨ _____

05 (their tent, us, lent, they, to)
⇨ _____

06 (his niece, taught, he, history, to)
⇨ _____

07 (her bike, she, to, him, sold)
⇨ _____

08 (a cake, we, her, made)
⇨ _____

09 (a chair, her, to, brought, my brother)
⇨ _____

10 (cooked, they, us, dinner)
⇨ _____

11 (of, a question, I, asked, her)
⇨ _____

12 (an email, I, wrote, her)
⇨ _____

1-5 5형식 [목적어 다음에 명사나 형용사가 나와 목적어의 신분이나 상태를 나타내는형식]

* She made **me** = a **coach**. [명사가 목적어의 신분을 나타냄]
* They found **her** = **happy**. [형용사가 목적의 상태를 나타냄]

01 The noise drove him **crazy**.

02 Those farmers made their land **green field**.

03 He painted the wall **green**.

04 I thought the plan unwise.

05 We consider the matter very important.

06 They found the man innocent.

07 We call him a walking dictionary.

08 This alarm system will keep our local hospital safe.

09 Your jacket will make you look more natural.

10 They say I'm too old, but I'm going to prove them all wrong.

11 I found my identification and a bag stolen last night.

12 Please don't leave any questions unanswered.

13 Mike set his goal too low. I think he needs some more encouragement.

14 Leave the boy alone so that he can make up his own mind.

15 A winner will make himself the owner of the sports car.

16 We believe competition between two groups unfair.

17 They finally found our products very useful for their customers.

18 He tried to make all the expressions simple and brief for children.

19 We believe our traditional dance the cultural heritage of Korea.

20 She considers using a cell phone in class disrespectful.

21 He called the birth of the poblic mechanical clock a turring point in westerm society.

Practice A

❖ **다음 빈칸에 알맞은 것을 고르시오.**

01 The party made her (happy / happily).

02 This food will keep you (health / healthy).

03 I found his life story (true / truly).

04 He solved the problem (easy / easily).

05 The built the bridge (strong / strongly).

06 She keeps her age (secret / secretly).

07 She cut my hair (strange / strangely).

08 Her smile made her (lovely / sweetly).

09 She made my birthday (special / specially).

10 He drives a car (careful / carefully).

11 I found this water (clean / cleanly).

12 Please leave me (alone / along).

13 You can set this plan (simple / simply).

14 He made everyone (quiet / quietly).

15 She kept her puppy (warm / warmly).

Chapter 2 조동사

2-1. can, be able to

She **can** be here on time.
We will **be able to** finish painting today.

2-2. may, might

He **may** be mad at me.
They **might** put this on their waist.

2-3. must, have to, should

You **must** be tired.
She **has to be** quiet.
You **should** take action.

2-4. 다양한 조동사 used to, had better, would rather

I **used to** eat a lot of ice cream.
She**'d better** stay home.
I **would rather** try anything than do nothing.

2-1 can [~할 수 있다, 해도 된다, ~일수도 있다.]

* I **can run** fast. (능력)
* You **can use** my computer. (허락)
* She **can be** a star. (가능성)
* I **was not able to** find a job in New York.

01 You **can enjoy** the autumn breeze starting tomorrow.

02 You **can't borrow** more money from John.

03 I **can lend** you enough money if you need more.

04 I**'ll be able to give** you a hand tomorrow.

05 Don't worry yourself about me, I can take care of myself.

06 Can you make a little less noise, please? I'm trying to work.

07 You can have a piece of cake after you've eaten your vegetables!

08 It can't be original design. I have seen many of those before.

09 He will be able to receive an award as the student of the year.

10 In the long term, alcohol can cause high blood pressure.

11 They can't be our ancestors. They are from another region.

12 If you feel more confident about yourself, you can overcome your shyness.

13 Science fiction movies can be used as an escape from reality.

14 Scientists still cannot explain exactly how the virus reproduces.

15 This program can translate your e-mail into other languages.

16 Mike is able to solve complicated math equations.

17 The support team will be able to help you in about ten minutes.

18 I won't be able to afford to buy you a car this summer.

19 You **can't be too** careful when choosing a friend. [아무리 ~해도 지나치지 않는]

20 Most accidents in the home **could** be prevented. [현재 예측 가능성]

2-2 may, might [~해도 된다, ~일지도 모른다.]

* You **may go** now. (허락)
* We **may not go** to the concert. (추측)
* We **might be** a few minutes late. (추측)

01 He **may calm** down if you apologize to him.

02 This kind of fish **might** only live in the west coast of Africa.

03 Accidents may occur if you are careless.

04 This illness may ruin her career.

05 She may not announce her wedding to them.

06 No one may own more than 10% of the land.

07 She might be able to find a useful source of information.

08 It might be a good idea to put those plants in the shade.

09 It may be spoiled if you put it outside.

10 There may be too many female teachers in elementary schools.

11 There may be another disaster if the weather forecast shows severe storms tonight.

12 He may take full responsibility for the accident.

13 The eggs may take four or five days to hatch.

14 A drought might force them to move to a different area.

15 The government may construct a new bridge over the river.

16 A crowd of reporters may gather outside the court today.

17 We might get there before it heavily rains.

18 The amount you save might be small, but it's still worth doing.

19 I may be new to this industry, but I have many relevant skills.

20 Activities, such as walking, standing, sitting or bending, may have to be learned anew.

2-3 must, have to [~해야만 한다, ~임에 틀림없다] should [~해야 한다: 당위성, 의무]

* You **must be** quiet. (금지)
* She **must be** genius. (추측)
* You **don't have to go** there. (~하지 않아도 된다)
* You **shouldn't lie**. (당위성)

01 Look at him. He **must be** in a bad mood.

02 You **must not touch** this wire.

03 You **have to react** quickly to circumsances.

04 Safety must be their chief concern.

05 His opinion must be opposite to mine.

06 No one must disturb him while he's sleeping.

07 Everything seems so expensive. There must be a sharp increase in price.

08 The angle between the walls and ceiling must be 45 degree.

09 There must be no proof that any creatures exist on Mars.

10 Her home must have a lovely and relaxed atmosphere.

11 You must pay attention to your teacher.

12 You must not forget the appointment with Mr. Johnson.

13 Passengers must present their tickets to the ticket officer.

14 You don't have to make another attempt to make people laugh.

15 If you earn more than $5,000, you will have to pay tax.

16 All children are equal, so every child must receive the same education.

17 He doesn't have to compete with others for her attention.

18 You don't have to refuse to answer his question.

19 We don't have to rush – there's plenty of time.

20 It doesn't have to be perfect as long as you try hard.

21 You need not water the plants today. I already did.

22 You need not worry that you don't know what you are doing.

23 Every sentence **should** start with a capital letter in English.

24 We should use fresh water instead of this liquid.

25 You should get some public opinions about your plan.

26 Privacy should be kept regardless of their age.

27 We should stop sacrificing everything we want to do for a later promise of happiness.

28 White wine, not red, should be served with fish.

29 The doctor said it will take six weeks to recover and I should be fine by then.

2-4 나도 조동사 [~하곤 했다, ~하는 편이 낫다, 차라리 ~하겠다.]

* I **used to** eat a lot of chocolate.
* You **had better** be quiet.
* I **would rather** give it up than waste time.

01 She **used to** be my rival at school.

02 You**'d better** stop tapping your feet!

03 I **would rather** deal with the problem than let someone else do it.

04 I used to dash into my room when I got upset.

05 She used to be certain about her future.

06 He used to study both politics and economics.

07 You'd better claim what you really need.

08 You'd better do something to improve the relationship.

09 You'd better not remind me of that painful memory.

10 I'd rather immigrate to America than live here.

11 I'd rather go sightseeing than stay in a hotel room.

Chapter 3 비교급, 원급 그리고 최상급

3-1. 비교급

She is **smarter than** my sister.

Time is **more important than** money.

We have **less money than** they do.

He became **fatter and fatter**.

The **higher** you fly, **the more** you can see.

3-2. 원급

She is **as rich as** I am.

I work **as hard as** you do.

This is **twice as big as** yours.

3-3. 최상급

Mike is **the smartest boy** of all.

This is **the most expensive watch** in this shop.

Who do you respect **most**?

3-1 비교급 [두 대상의 우열 비교를 나타내는 표현]

> * 단어에 모음이 하나만 있는 경우에 단어 끝에 ~er을 붙인다.
>   fast, big, tall, strong, smart, high
>
> * 모음이 두 개지만 발음이 하나로 되면 ~er을 붙인다.
>   early, easy, quiet, strange, large, simple, gentle, close
>
> * 단어에 모음이 두 개 혹은 그 이상 있는 경우 앞에 more 를 붙입니다.
>   important → more important   honest - more honest
>
> * 양을 나타내는 경우에는 more, less를 사용한다.
>
> * 비교급 형태가 완전히 바뀌는 경우 good - better   bad - worse   far - farther

01 An electric lamp is **brighter than** a lamp.
　　　　　　　　　　　　　　　보다

02 This piece of wood is thicker than that.

03 Your cap is cheaper than that red one.

04 The lake has become shallower than last year.

05 The developer is cleverer than that.

06 Is this dress available in a larger size?

07 Fewer participants will volunteer for the study than I expected.

08 Sam is **more intelligent than** his brother.

09 My bike has more potential power than yours.

10 This is a more complicated voting system than before.

11 Business school was less expensive than law school.

12 The violence was worse than we expected.

13 We now have a **much** better understanding of the disease. [비교급 강조: far, a lot, even, still]

14 This place has even more relaxed atmosphere than the one we visited.

15 They have tried to save **more and more** money for the homeless. [more and more: 점점 더]

16 This shop is getting more and more crowded.

17 **The more** successful he became, **the less** happy he felt. [the more, the more: ~할수록 더]

18 The more educated women are, the later they marry.

19 The more carefully you plan, the better the result will be.

3-2 원급 비교 [두 대상이 양이나 질에서 같은 것을 표현하며 뒤에 as만 ~만큼이라고 해석]

* Mike is **as old as** my sister.
* Sarah runs **as fast as** you.
* We ate **as much as** they did.

01 She is **as busy as** bee.
　　　　　　　　만큼

02 Mike is **as brave as** bull.

03 The world's biggest bull is as big as a small elephant.

04 The weather this summer is as humid as last year.

05 You should drive your dad's car as carefully as you can.

06 Brian is as humble as all the other his friends.

07 We did not enjoy the pasta dish as much as the rice dish.

08 He doesn't earn as much money as his brother.

09 This phone doesn't have as many features as the other one.

10 It's as good as you can get for the price.

11 My ticket cost twice as much as yours.

3-3 최상급 [장소나 무리에서 가장 으뜸인 경우에 사용]

> *최상급을 만드는 방법은 비교급과 같으면 단어 끝에 -est를 혹은 단어 앞에 most를 붙이며 범위를 한정 해 주는 of, in 과 같이 사용된다.
>
> old - oldest   smart - smartest   honest - most honest   dangerous - most dangerous

01 My house is **the largest one in** our neighborhood.

02 Kevin is **the smartest boy of** them.

03 This is the most precious experience I have ever had.

04 Mike gave me the most valuable lesson in my life.

05 I am hungriest after watching ads for pizza.

06 We shall find out which system works most effectively.

07 She is one of the politest people I have ever met.

08 This is the least expensive sweater in the store.

09 Peter was wearing the most ridiculous costume at the Halloween party.

10 When you consider all of the insects in our garden, the ladybugs have been the least destructive.

11 It will take you **at least** 20 minutes to get there. [적어도, 최소한]

영어를 말로 하고 안 하고의 차이점

우리 모두는 중학교 때 비교급을 배운다.

She is taller than me.

I got up earlier than you.

우리는 비교급 만드는 방법을 주로 해석하는 것을 목적 위주로 배운다.
문법을 배우면 영작을 해 보지도 않고 말로도 거의 안 한다.

아주 오래전에 원어민하고 대화를 하다 한 가지 이상한 점을 발견했다.

나와 만나기로 했던 원어민이 **I got here earlier than she did.** 라고 말을 했다.

내가 알기로는 **I got here earlier than her.** 라고 해야 했는데

궁금한 것을 못 참았던 나는 다음 날 학교에 가서 교수님에게 질문했다.

그 교수님은 다음 문장을 읽어 보라고 했다.

I got here earlier than her.

나는 힘차게 읽어 보았는데, 그 교수님은 보통 문장을 읽거나 말을 하는 경우
항상 끝이 내려가게 되어 있는데 대명사인 her가 문장 끝에 나오면 끝이 올라가게 된다고 말했다.

그래서 나는 다시 읽어 보았지만 역시 her를 읽는 순간 나도 모르게 문장 끝이 올라갔다.
끝이 올라가면 질문 형식이라서 다시 내려서 읽으려고 해도 안 내려갔다.

아! 그렇구나. 속으로만 읽었지, 실제 말로 내뱉으면서 읽어 본 적이 거의 없다 보니.

그리고 문장에 주어가 주격인 "I" 라서 같은 비교 대상 주격 she라고 해야 한다고 하는데
이것은 문장 구성상 다양한 주장이 있다.

어쨌든

You are busier than I am.

You are busier than me.

두 문장을 읽어 보고 차이점을 확인 해 보시기 바랍니다.

Chapter 4 시제

4-1. 현재 (사실이나, 습관, 진리 등을 표현할 때 사용)

7 times 7 **is** 49.
We **get** together once a month.
The sun **rises** in the east and sets in the west.

Practice A [현재 동사]

4-2. 현재 완료 (과거에 발생해서 현재와 관련 있는 상황에 사용)

She **has seen** her once.
We **have just begun** the course.
They **have helped** us since last year.
Mike **has gone** to Paris.

Practice A, B [have + p. p]

4-3. 과거 완료 (과거에 두 가지 일이 발생 한 경우 앞 뒤 선후를 구별하는 경우)

We found that she **had missed** her flight.
When we got to the airport, the flight **had already taken** off.

Practice A [had + p. p]

4-1 현재 시제 [현재의 사실, 습관, 진리를 나타내는 현재 시제]

* She **is** a honest worker. (사실)
* I **go** to bed early. (습관)
* The sun **rises** in the east. (진리)

01 Some people feel proud of themselves, others don't.

02 My main concern is your health and future.

03 People gather together to take a picture at a wedding.

04 Some companies advertise their products only on Sunday.

05 She describes him as a danger to our society.

06 He needs a small metal object for the shelves.

07 It takes a lot of time and effort to get a good result.

08 I often increase my studying time to get a good result on the test.

09 Mike always takes great pride in himself.

10 She claims to be a descendent of Charles Dickens

11 **Are** you still **receiving** financial aid? (현재 진행형)

12 Most people spend nearly a third of their lives asleep.

13 Alex interacts well with other children in the class.

14 According to wise men throughout the years, decreasing your desires is a sure way to happiness.

15 If he **falls** asleep, pour some cold water on his face. (조건 접속사 if 다음이 미래라도 현재 시간을 사용)

16 If you try to float, you will rather sink.

17 If you don't understand the question, I can repeat it for you.

18 **As** you **long as** you are polite to them, you won't be in trouble. (~하는 한)

19 I can't leave her **unless** I know she's all right. (~하지 않는 한)

20 When you **rush**, you will always make a mistake. (시간 접속사 다음이 미래라도 현재 시간을 사용)

21 When you reach the first destination, I will tell you another direction.

22 When he makes an apology, you should accept it.

23 After you finish your homework, your mother will allow you to go out.

24 Bend your knees two or three times before you stretch.

25 **Once** I get him a job, he will be fine. (일단 ~하면)

26 It is undesirable to express one's opinion while he is hiding his identity.

27 While the population of the world is growing rapidly, it is not growing at the same rate in all regions.

Practice A

❖ 다음 알맞은 동사를 고르시오.

01 When she (comes, will come) here, I will buy her dinner.

02 If she (will get, gets) angry, she throws everything.

03 Don't come before you (will finish, finish) the work.

04 I will go home after I (meet, will meet) her.

05 Will you tell me when you (get, will get) the money?

06 They (won't leave, don't leave) if they (won't get, don't get) the money.

07 I (will invite, invite) my friends when I (will be, am) ready.

08 They (will be, are) happy if I (will give, give) them a cake.

09 Mike always helps others when he (will have, has) free time.

10 We can't do it if she (won't help, doesn't help) us.

11 Jenny will buy a gift for me when she (gets, will get) money from her mom.

12 I don't know when he (brings, will bring) my bike.

13 They are going to stay in the hotel if they (get, will get) more free time.

14 Mike wants to travel to Europe when he (gets, will get) a vacation.

4-2 현재 완료 [과거에 발생한 일이 현재까지 영향을 미치는 경우]
[경험, 완료, 계속, 결과]

* She **has never been** to London. (경험)
* We **have just had** lunch. (완료)
* He **has known** her for 10 years. (계속)
* They **have gone** to Paris. (결과)

01 She **has never been** to any other foreign countries except Japan.

02 I **have just been** to the store to buy groceries.

03 He **has already expressed** his feelings about her.

04 She has demanded equal and fair treatment since she started working here.

05 Towns and cities all over the country have been flooded.

06 We have made a lot of effort to achieve our goal.

07 We have studied hard to gain not only knowledge but also wisdom.

08 She has gone to the desert to study new species.

09 He has taken a deep breath and he is now ready to jump off the cliff.

10 She has created a new kind of music since she was 30 years old.

11 We have seen many amazing skyscrapers in this city.

12 Your mission has been successful and I am proud of your accomplishment.

13 The police have just arrived at the crime scene.

14 She has voluntarily worked for charity since last year.

15 The material has been available for the past 3 years.

16 I have offered him a nice job, but I think he may refuse it.

17 We have done many simple experiments on athletes.

18 He has played an important role in his family.

19 She is the most courageous woman I have ever seen.

20 Has she obtained enough information about recent technology?

21 She has finally examined all the evidence since she came here.

22 Unfortunately, they haven't produced quality goods yet.

23 We have judged people by their appearance.

24 She has taken advantage of good weather since she got there.

25 He has done many things to approach a normal life.

26 You have gone too far. I mean you have crossed the line.

Practice A

❖ 괄호 안에서 알맞은 것을 고르시오.

01 My father has just (come, came) home.

02 When (did you go, have you gone) to the museum?

03 Kevin (stayed, has stayed) here since last Monday.

04 She (went, has gone) to London last week.

05 We (have been, have gone) to New York before.

06 It (rained, has rained) for three days.

07 Her father (died, has died) long ago.

08 She (didn't, hasn't) done his homework yet.

09 I (lost, have lost) my bag. I can't find it.

10 She (left, has left) for Hong Kong last week.

11 He (has been, has gone) to the museum. He is now sleeping.

12 He (has been, has gone) to the museum. He will be here late at night.

13 She has lived here (for, since) two years.

14 She has known him (for, since) last year.

15 He has worked for her (for, since) the past two years.

4-3 과거 완료 [과거에 발생한 두 개의 일 중에 더 먼저 일어난 일을 had p. p로]

* I **had seen** you before you saw me.
* Susie went to lunch after she **had finished** her work.

01 I **washed** the floor when the painter **had gone**.

02 I didn't say anything until she **had finished** talking.

03 By the time he phoned her, she **had found** someone new.

04 We looked for witnesses, but the neighbors had not seen anything unusual.

05 The concert had already started when we entered the stadium.

06 Sam hadn't had time to explain his side of the story before he got to London.

07 Had Adam ever spoken to the CEO before he was fired?

08 Simon had not been expecting a positive answer when he got a job.

09 How long had he driven before the accident occurred?

10 The hikers hadn't been walking long before they got lost.

Practice A

❖ 다음 중 옳은 것을 고르시오.

01 A bus (has left / had left) already when I got to the bus stop.

02 She (has had / had had) the watch over past 10 years.

03 Before 20 year-old, she (has been / had been) to Africa three times.

04 I (have had / had had) a lot of money before I lent him.

05 How long (have you / had you) worked here before you quit?

06 He has to give up buying a house because he (has spent / had spent) the money.

07 When she finished her dinner, she found that everyone in her office (has left / had left).

08 She (has been / had been) in Japan for more than ten years.

09 It (has rained / had rained) a lot right before you came here.

10 I found that someone (has taken / had taken) my computer.

11 We (have tried / had tried) to ride a bike a few times before.

12 They (have arrived / had arrived) at the house before we cleaned the mess.

13 She saw the movie which we (have seen / had seen).

14 I realized that they (have / had) used my computer without telling me.

15 He (has been / had been) in a pro team since I married him.

확실히 알고 가기! few / little

a. little or a little

보통 학생들에게 little의 뜻에 대해 질문하면, 조금이요, 약간이요 라고 하는 경우가 많습니다.
학생들이 알고 있는 약간, 조금의 의미는 a little이고 little은 [거의 없는] 의 의미를 가지고 있습니다.

셀 수 없는 단어가 나와야 하는 a little은 다음에 money가 나오면 약간의 돈을 의미하고
크기에서의 작다는 의미로 사용되는 경우에는 a little girl, a little house와 같이 셀 수 있는 명사가 나오는
경우도 있으며, 이때는 small이라는 의미와 비슷하게 사용됩니다.

little은 부정의 의미를 가지고 있으며,

Many of the students speak little or no English. [동사를 부정으로 해석해야 합니다.]
  학생들의 많은 수가 영어를 거의 못하거나 아예 못한다.

She paid little attention to my class.
  그녀는 거의 집중하지 않았다 나의 수업에

01 She gets very angry over little things. [사소한 것들]

02 I'm feeling a little tired, I think I'll go upstairs and have a rest.

03 I just have a little information about this kind of material.

04 His work has improved a little since he began the special classes.

05 We'll have to wait a little longer to see what happens.

06 There is little chance of success.

07 She has done little to improve her performance on the stage.

08 I know little or nothing about fixing computers.

b. few or a few

a few는 다음에 a few questions 와 같이 **셀 수 있는** 명사가 나오며, 다음에 나오는 명사에 따라 "몇" 사람, 몇 가지 등으로 해석할 수 있습니다.

A few of them agreed to my plan.
  그들 중 몇 명이 나의 계획에 동의했다.

그러나 few는 **거의 없는** 이란 의미로 사용되며, 주로 형식적인 표현에서 많이 사용됩니다.

Few of them agreed to my plan.
그들 중 나의 계획에 동의한 사람이 거의 없다.

동사를 부정으로 해석하며 few나 little은 부정어와 같이 사용할 수 없습니다.

01 He called me a few days later.

02 Few people knew he was ill.

03 A few of my friends came to help me.

04 There are a few places you can visit while you are here.

05 She asked me a few questions that I couldn't answer.

06 She was in trouble, but few were willing to help.

07 Few students paid attention to his class.

08 This is the job that few people want.

Chapter 5 to-부정사

5-1. 명사로 쓰이는 to-부정사 [~하는 것, ~하기를]

To work with her is fun.
My dream is **to be** an astronaut.
She wants **to be** a leader.

5-2. 형용사로 to-부정사 [~할]

I have someone **to meet** today.
They need a book **to read**.

5-3. 부사로 to-부정사 [~하기 위해, ~해서, ~하기에, ~하고나서]

She left early **to catch** the flight.
I felt sorry **to make** a mistake.
This is hard **to break**.
He grew up **to be** a judge.
in order to, so ~ that [~하기 위하여]

5-4. 사역동사, 지각동사 [make, have, let, help] [see, feel, watch, hear..]

I **made** her **leave** early.
We **let** her **stay** at our place.
I **saw** her **jump** off the cliff.
We **felt** someone **pushing** us.

5-5. too ~ to   [~해서 ~할 수 없는]
형 + enough + to   [~할 정도로 ~하는]

She is **too** selfish **to** make friends.
We are **strong enough to** beat them.

5-1 명사 자리에 나오는 경우 [~것, ~하기를]

* **To go** to bed early is a good habit.
* My hope is **to be** rich.
* I decided not **to help** her.
* She asked me **to join** the club.
* We decided what **to do** today.

01 **To work with** him is very comfortable. (주어)

02 **To join this tennis club** is not easy.

03 It is impossible **to find** this kind of material in Korea. (가주어)

04 It is right to treat people equally.

05 It is the custom to obey our parents in Korea.

06 It is a little difficult to understand the local dialect.

07 It is the joy of my life to look after my daughter.

08 It depends on your effort to pass the test.

09 It is hard to recognize someone if you haven't seen him or her for a long time.

10 It is hard to gain a reputation but is easy to ruin.

11 My job today is **to find an expert** in this field. (보어)

12 Her duty is to check every item before Mike delivers them.

13 My wish is to achieve my goal of becoming a movie star.

14 The purpose of this meeting is to elect a new leader.

15 She hopes **to get along with** her new friends. (목적어)

16 She needs to develop a positive mental attitude.

17. He wants to buy a certain gift for his children before he leaves.

18 She planned to delay her trip to New York due to illness.

19 Jenny suddenly appeared and demanded to know what was going on.

20 Everyone promised to keep silent including Mike.

21 How do you **manage to work** in this heat without air conditioning?

22 We are not related we just **happened to have** the similar name.

23 I need you **to give** me some basic information about the climate here. (목적 보어)

24 He asked me to give him an exact amount of money.

25 I never expected this simple mistake to destroy the environment.

26 I advised him not to accept her offer.

27 The warmer temperatures caused the ice caps to melt.

28 We do not allow people to smoke anywhere in the building.

29 She told us **how to find** a right computer for children like us. (의문사 + to 부정사)

30 I'll tell you what to do to destroy cockroaches in your house.

5-2 형용사 역할을 하는 [명사 뒤에 나와서 앞에 명사를 꾸며주는 역할, ~할]

* I have something **to tell** you. (말할 것)
* We need more food **to eat**. (먹을 음식)

01 I need someone **to depend on** while going to college.

02 You have to find someone **to train** this wild bear.

03 He needs money **to buy** a book.

04 He is not the man to manage our store.

05 She told me a way to increase crop production.

06 I will give you five more minutes to explain yourself.

07 Perhaps, she has something to discuss with you.

08 It is time for us to arrange another trip for them.

09 She has an ability to encourage her students to study hard.

10 This is the man to help you improve your English ability.

11 The movie to watch tomorrow with John is Interstellar.

12 She showed me something to sell at the flea market.

13 Brian made an attempt to win for the team.

14 There is a huge demand for new cars to drive long distances.

15 We should set new rules to prevent accidents.

16 The girl to choose to be your girlfriend is Sarah.

17 You can trust him. He is not a person to betray you.

18 Step back, leave room for people to get past.

19 The goal is to improve the company's ability to compete.

20 The desire to succeed motivated him to work harder.

21 I have nothing left to fear.

5-3 부사 역할을 하는 [형용사나 부사 혹은 동사를 수식: ~하기 위하여, ~해서, ~하기가, and]

* He felt sorry **to ruin** the party. (~해서)
* This is difficult **to use**. (~하기가)
* She woke **to see** Brian standing by the window. (and)
* She left early **to catch** the train. (위하여)
* Sam trained every day **in order to** improve his performance. (so as ~ to, so that S+V)

01 This chemical is dangerous **to treat**. (~하기가, ~하기에)

02 This kind of problem is difficult **to correct**.

03 Activities such as hiking and climbing are fun to try.

04 She made every step hard to handle.

05 His offer is not easy to refuse.

06 My boss is impossible to please.

07 This bottled water is safe to drink.

08 I looked at the answer sheet **to find** correct answers. (~하기 위하여)

09 We went to the airport to greet our new guests.

10 To find out more about university courses, write to this address.

11 Put this ice around your neck to lower your body temperature.

12 Can you measure the desk to see if it'll fit into that corner?

13 The police surrounded the house to arrest a criminal.

14 He used a brush to get rid of stains on the carpet.

15 We decided to stay in a motel to reduce travel expenses.

16 Most people do things to impress others, not to make them happy.

17 He is working day and night to launch an application.

18 She started taking a deep breath to calm herself down.

19 To create something that we can be proud of later in life, we are working tirelessly.

20 I entered the house quietly **in order not to** frighten anyone.

21 I moved slowly forward **so as not to** disturb anyone in the group.

22 Why don't you start out early **so that** you don't have to hurry?

23 Steps must be taken **so that** this kind of disaster never happens again.

24 Samuel trained every day **in order that** he could improve his performance.

25 I was angry **to lose** my temper while talking to Jenny. (~해서, ~때문에)

26 She felt disappointed to hear her son give up the contest.

27 I felt sorry to see many homeless people on the street.

28 I was embarrassed to find my son sleeping in class.

29 They were pleased to be invited to your party.

30 She woke **to see** Ben standing by the window. (to = and)

31 He arrived there to find that the last train had already left.

32 **To be honest** (= speaking honestly), Becky, I like the grey shirt better. (독립 부정사)

33 It was totally unnecessary, **to begin with**. (우선, 말하자면)

Practice A

❖ 다음 문장을 해석할 경우에 해당되는 적합한 의미를 고르시오.

> **a.** ~하기 위해 **b.** ~해서 (~ 때문에) **c.** ~하기가 (~하기에) **d.** ~할 **e.** ~하는 것은

01 This sofa is comfortable to sit on.

02 We came here early to meet John.

03 This river is dangerous to swim in.

04 I took a bus to go to the library.

05 I was angry to fail the test.

06 Harry told me not to open the box.

07 I was glad to meet a new friend.

08 This math question was hard to understand.

09 They are happy to buy a new house.

10 She decided not to help her.

11 We were sad to hear the news.

12 The mountain is difficult to climb.

13 He has something to tell you.

14 I want you to leave now.

15 It is not easy to solve the problem.

5-4 사역동사, 지각동사 [make, have, let, help] [see, feel, watch, hear...]

* We made her **clean** the house.
* I let her **ride** my bike.
* We found Sam **sitting** on the bench.
* Jack saw Jim **get** on the bus.
* I heard my name **called**.

01 She **made** me **stay** calm and say nothing.

02 He didn't **let** me **change** the way I look.

03 My father **had** me **sit** beside him.

04 What makes you think I am not like you?

05 My mother didn't let me hang out with Mike.

06 We couldn't make her challenge the contest.

07 I will have her follow our traditions and customs.

08 I will not let anyone damage your personal property.

09 Please let him do his job without any disturbance.

10 She had her tooth pulled out.

11 She had her masterpiece displayed at the gallery.

12 She **felt** something **crawling** on her leg. [지각동사]

13 We **saw** the building **destroyed** in an earthquake.

14 He **noticed** a man in black **sitting** across from him.

15 I found my patient suffering from lack of sleep.

16 It is pleasant to see some poor people benefit from the government.

17 I watched them supply fresh water to people in need.

18 I heard her invade your privacy.

19 I noticed some customers complaining about your service.

20 I found this ancient palace built back in the 1300s.

21 I heard the teacher who looked angry asking Mike not to be absent from class.

22 I saw someone I met this morning sitting in the shade of a big tree.

Practice A

❖ 다음 빈 칸에 알맞은 형태를 고르시오. (사역동사)

01 She asked his brother (do / doing / to do) the dishes for her.

02 I got them (to be / be / being) in line straight.

03 She helped a stranger (look for / to look for) the way to the museum.

04 Peter made them (to stay / stay) quiet all the time.

05 I let my son (to watch / watch) TV for 2 hours.

06 They wanted the students (to help / help) the old lady.

07 We had her (to buy / buy) some snacks for the children.

08 Sam expected them (to take / take) the medicine three times a day.

09 I tried to have my puppy (wait / to wait) for the food I give her.

10 She made some cake (to give / give) her boy friend.

11 Your kind smile made them (to come / come) to your shop again.

12 She allowed us (to use / use) her computer all day.

13 We told us (to sell / sell) our bikes at a low price.

14 I let Chris (to ride / ride) my bike to school tomorrow.

15 What made them (to fight / fight) with each other?

❖ 다음 주어진 단어를 이용하여 빈칸을 채우시오. (답이 2개 있는 경우도 있음: 지각동사)

01 I saw your dog _____ my shoes. (bite)

02 I advised her _____ harder. (study)

03 He wants you _____ here tonight. (stay)

04 He made her son _____ out of the house. (go)

05 Mike told me _____ exercise every day. (do)

06 I felt someone _____ my shoulder. (touch)

07 He had his son _____ the boxes. (carry)

08 I saw Mike _____ with his friend. (argue)

09 I heard my phone _____. (ring)

10 She had her car _____. (wash)

11 He helped me _____ the test. (pass)

12 He allowed me _____ her. (meet)

13 She let me _____ her computer. (use)

14 She ordered me _____ calm. (remain)

15 I heard her _____ in the bathroom. (sing)

❖ 다음 중 틀린 문장을 수정하시오.

01 She watched his son played baseball.

02 We would like Mike join the club to get some discount.

03 Mike felt some stranger carried his backpack.

04 No one could find someone to steal his bag.

05 I saw a few birds to fly over my house.

06 We heard John and David to sing on the stage.

07 I heard him made her cooking dinner for the students.

08 Mike had her son reading the book loudly.

09 They got their students without umbrellas wait for their parents.

10 Did you feel the ground to shake for a second?

11 It is hard to hear him to speaking on the phone.

12 The movie he saw last night made him crying.

13 I watched the ice cream on his hand kept melting.

5-5 too~to [너무 ~해서 ~할 수 없다] 형용사+enough + to [~할 정도로 ~하다]

* You are **too young to go** to school.
* She is **old enough to** ride the roller coaster.
* It is not easy **for us** to carry the table. [의미상의 주어]
* It is stupid **of me** to believe her.

01 He is **too careless to avoid** making mistakes.

02 His disease is too serious to recover.

03 She is too greedy to give up the rest of the food.

04 This lake is too shallow to swim in.

05 He was too humble to boast about his success.

06 I was too shameful to ask him for more money.

07 The rooms are all **large enough to take** a third bed.

08 She is attractive enough to draw our attention.

09 I am not foolish enough to lend him the money.

10 He is generous enough to forgive you.

11 My father is **so** strict **that** I **can't** bring my friends home.

12 He is **so familiar** with this area that he **can** tell where everything is.

13 She was so frustrated that she couldn't want to keep studying.

14 The air was so smoky that it was difficult to breathe.

15 The weather is not so mild that you can seldom see any tourists in the area.

16 His schedule is so irregular that I can't make an appointment with him.

17 It is polite **of you** to show me the directions.　[의미상의 주어]

18 It is impossible **for us** to solve the problem.

19 It is difficult for her to refuse his offer.

20 It is brave of you to accept his challenge.

21 It is rude of him to talk back to his teacher.

Chapter 6 동명사 [동사에 ~ing를 붙여 명사로 사용, ~하는 것]

6-1. 동명사

* **주어**
  Teaching is fun.
  Raising children is fun.

* **보어 자리**
  Her job is **building** houses.
  Her dream is **being** an artist.

* **목적어 자리에**
  She enjoys **listening** to music.
  He finished **cleaning** the house.

* **전치사 다음에**
  I am proud of **being** an army officer.
  I'm interested in **learning** Japanese.

* **행태가 갖춰진 구**
  We feel like **going** out tonight.
  It is worthless **fixing** this bike.

  Practice A, B

6-1 동명사 [~ing를 붙여 동사 기능을 갖는 명사로 사용]

* **Swimming** is a great exercise. (주어)
* My hobby is **listening** to music. (보어)
* I enjoying **teaching**. (목적어)
* Would you like to walk instead of **taking** the bus? (전치사 다음에)

01 **Biking** is my newest hobby. (주어)

02 **Living** a life in a cage is sad.

03 Growing this plant in hot climates is impossible.

04 Discovering a new land was a sailor's job.

05 Being a politician in Korea is not a good idea.

06 Learning foreign languages and cultures is fun and interesting.

07 Attending college costs a lot of money.

08 Responding to your email immediately is not my duty.

09 Earning enough income will make your family feel happy.

10 Setting up a satellite system costs a lot of money.

11 Paying particular attention to spelling during a test is important.

12 Sowing the seeds one inch deep in the soil brings early crops.

13 Being able to concentrate on one thing is a good habit.

14 Failing something means you will get another chance to succeed.

15 My hobby is **reading** romantic novels. (보어)

16 My dream is being an astronaut.

17 Her hope is finding a nest for her pet bird to lay its eggs.

18 My plan this year is making a lot of money.

19 A way to clear your mind is taking a walk in nature.

20 He gave up **raising** rare birds in his house. (목적어)

21 We finished baking several cakes for the homeless.

22 Many Korean people began settling down in Argentina.

23 My employer often delays paying his bills.

24 She denied seeing me at the party.

25 I appreciate your helping me meet my goal.

26 They are considering accepting my offer.

27 Mike avoids talking to Jenny about their marriage.

28 We stopped **drinking** soda while working out.

*29 We stopped **to discuss** the matter in a productive way. (비교)

30 I remember **meeting** her at a party once.

*31 Don't forget **to check** your luggage. (forget to / remember ~ing: 할 것, 한 것)

32 She is good at **communicating** with foreigners. (전치사 다음에)

33 What is the purpose of visiting our town?

34 I'm interested in increasing the value of my house.

35 I am proud of being a member of your club.

36 She is responsible for handling an emergency case.

37 She is thinking of retiring from her job this year.

38 Instead of decreasing the speed, he stopped the car.

39 Thanks for replacing the batteries in my clock.

40 You will have a chance of advancing to a higher level next month.

41 We should start by electing a new leader.

42 I don't **feel like adding** chemicals to make it more tastier. (형태가 갖춰진 문장)

43 It's no use making a decision now. It's too late.

44 It's worthless including him as our player. We will lose anyway.

45 I'm looking forward to seeing all of my close relatives soon.

46 I spent this afternoon burying my lovely puppy.

47 The barrier is to **prevent** people **from coming** in without a visa. (keep, stop)

48 I couldn't help laughing at her negative attitude.

*49 Lee could not help but agree with her.

50 We got used to dealing with this kind of problem.

*51 This material is used to prevent fire from happening.

*52 He used to lose his temper quite often.

Practice A

❖ **Complete the sentences using the given words.**

01 _____ is good for health. (walk)

02 _____ English is important. (speak)

03 _____ soccer is fun. (play)

04 My hobby is _____ foreign coins. (collect)

05 My dream is _____ my own car. (have)

06 I finished _____ my car. (wash)

07 She enjoys _____ children. (teach)

08 He is interested in _____. (paint)

09 I want _____ a bike for my son. (buy)

10 _____ is my favorite hobby. (go fishing)

11 I'm good at _____ the piano. (play)

12 She is afraid of _____ mistakes. (make)

13 Mike gave up _____ her English. (teach)

14 I didn't mind _____ for you. (wait)

15 Susie is worried about _____ the test. (fail)

Practice B

❖ **Complete the sentences using the given words.**

01 I feel like _____ to music. (listen)

02 She will go _____ if she feels bored. (swim)

03 He may be busy _____ history. (study)

04 He doesn't mind _____ her to the party. (invite)

05 She can spend 30 minutes _____ bread. (bake)

06 She expects _____ her grandson. (look after)

07 I am looking forward to _____ you soon. (see)

08 I am proud of _____ your student. (be)

09 It is worthless _____ him how to swim. (teach)

10 She couldn't help _____ her job. (give up)

11 I'm not afraid of _____ the test. (fail)

12 I'm sure of _____ tomorrow. (leave)

13 She is interested in _____ foreigners. (meet)

14 _____ a promise is very important. (keep)

15 She kept _____ until her mother came. (cry)

Chapter 7 수동태 [주어에 동작이 가해지는 형식: be + p. p]

7-1. 기본 형태

She **was invited** to the party.
I **was taken** to the hospital.

Practice A. B

7-2. 조동사가 나오는 수동태

This town **may be flooded**.
It **must be writhe**n in red.

Practice A. B. C

7-3. 5형식이 수동태 되면 2형식으로

She **was made** happy.
He **is called** Jack.

7-4. by가 없거나 덩어리로 나오는 수동태

We **were surprised** at the news.
She **is taken care of by** her aunt.

Practice A

7-1 수동태 [be + P. P : 주어에 동작이 가해지는 문장 형식]

* She **was invited** to the party.
* They **are not sold** here.

01 He **was given** some jewelry by his bride.

02 Your parcel **was sent** to England yesterday.

03 This building **was designed** by a famous professor.

04 A few employees were fired last week because of their laziness.

05 Two criminals were seen at the department store.

06 This movie was not made by that director.

07 I was sent a precious photo from my sister.

08 Rainwater is used for watering the grass around the building.

09 His painting was shown to everyone in class.

10 These articles were written by an architect.

11 The vase was placed by the window.

12 Ceilings were lowered and rooms look smaller.

13 This architecture was built 100 years ago.

14 The seed of its plant was brought into Korea in 12 century.

15 Their eyes were focused on his strange behavior.

16 The warning sign is usually written in red and yellow.

17 The cause of the fire was not determined.

18 The earth is divided into six different continents.

19 This castle was destroyed by the recent earthquake.

20 Her coffee was spilt on her skirt.

21 The test was predicted to be difficult.

22 Meat was preferred at the party.

23 My hometown is located in central New York.

24 Millions of elderly people are led to live in poverty.

25 He was buried on the edge of the forest.

26 The crime rate was reduced last year.

27 For decades, most of the relief work was done by volunteers.

28 The conflict was caused by cultural differences between our two societies.

29 She was educated in England and immigrated to the U.S.

30 My money was refunded when there was no sign of using the product.

31 The country was invaded and occupied by England in 16th century.

Practice A

❖ 다음 알맞은 것을 고르시오.

01 She (invited / was invited) her friend to the party.

02 He (gave / was given) money by John.

03 She (made / was made) happy.

04 This cat (caught / was caught) in the trap last night.

05 She (took / was taken) to the hospital.

06 Her mother (saw / was seen) at the post office.

07 She (drove / was driven) to New York by him.

08 This dog (bit / was bitten) by another dog.

09 He (invited / was invited) to the party.

10 He (took / was taken) her to the hospital.

11 This house (built / was built) in 2006.

12 The store (closed / was closed) last week.

13 This bus (hit / was hit) my little puppy.

14 The money (spent / was spent) for the orphans.

15 We (built / are built) the bridge this year.

❖ 다음 동사를 이용하여 문장을 완성하시오.

01 This jacket _____ last week. (buy)

02 The thief _____ yesterday. (catch)

03 The cake _____ by him today. (bring)

04 My purse _____ last night. (steal)

05 She _____ this machine for us last year. (invent)

06 This pie _____ by her every day. (make)

07 He _____ English last year. (teach)

08 They _____ into the ship by her this morning. (carry)

09 We _____ to the museum by him. (drive)

10 The doors _____ green yesterday. (paint)

11 The letter _____ in red by her today. (write)

12 She _____ by a policeman. (stop)

13 This bike _____ last year. (buy)

14 Her mother _____ alone on weekends. (leave)

15 He _____ math by her mother every day. (teach)

7-2 조동사가 나오는 수동태 [조동사 + be + p. p]

* She **will be forgiven**.
* This bike **can't be repaired**.
* It **must be done** today.

01 The rules **must be followed** by all students.

02 A wild animal **shouldn't be raised** at home.

03 In general, all passengers **will be guided** to the main gate.

04 This man will be led to heaven.

05 Germs must be killed if you want to keep your bathroom clean.

06 The problems can only be solved by an expert.

07 Can it be cooked without a proper recipe?

08 You have to be prepared for the competition.

09 Some faithful employees will be invited to the party.

10 Your offer will be refused by my boss.

11 The whole park will be spoiled by trash.

12 Stars in the sky can't be observed in a big city.

13 Your portrait will be drawn by my niece.

14 The whole healing process will be shown to his parents.

15 Passengers should be reminded to board the plane with their passport.

16 You might be given a false name and address, please chect it out.

17 Infants should be fed with mother's milk within an hour of birth.

18 Lung cancer can't be cured if it is not discovered at an early stage.

19 Proper action should be taken before it gets worse.

20 A reasonable level of physical fitness should be maintained all the time.

Practice A

❖ **다음을 수동태로 전환하시오.**

01 She will show us another movie.

= Another movie _____ by her.

02 Mike should find a job soon.

= _____ by Mike.

03 We couldn't solve the problem.

= The problem _____ by us.

04 She may drive us to Seoul.

= We _____

05 They might not take the children to the amusement park.

= _____

06 People must not cause such problems.

= Such problems _____

07 You shouldn't expect a better result.

= A better result _____

08 You have to do this work now.

= This work _____ by you.

09 She must press the button right now.

= A button _____ by her.

10 A waiter will serve the tea to everyone in the room.

= The tea _____ in the room by a waiter.

Practice B

❖ 다음을 수동태로 전환하시오.

01 Will you bring that chair to me?

= _____

02 Can you prepare dinner for us?

= _____

03 Did he buy this cake?

= _____

04 Should I choose one of them?

= _____

05 Does she have to change the curtains?

= _____

06 He didn't eat that cake.

= _____

07 The police may want the man.

= _____

08 Who wrote this on the wall?

= _____

09 His words didn't make her angry.

= _____

10 When will you repair my bike?

= _____

Practice C

❖ **다음 중 틀린 문장을 수정하시오.**

01 She may be showed another program.

02 They must be surprised in her talent.

03 Another gift will be given Mike.

04 A great car should find for his father.

05 Does the door must be opened door every day?

06 She should invite to the party.

07 A cake will send to her on her birthday.

08 Her table may cover with a lot of food.

09 She will see in the dark if she wears this vest.

10 Mike may be laughed by her friends.

11 Jenny's old car will sell at a high price.

12 Can be he sent some money for food?

13 Her expensive ring may be stole if she leaves it on the table.

14 Tell me why she lost on the way.

15 Trash may be not thrown at beach any more.

7-3 5형식이 수동태 되면 2형식으로

* We call him Jack. = He **is called** Jack. [He=Jack]
* He made her happy. = She **was made** happy by him. [She=happy]

01 He is called **a walking encyclopedia**.

02 The sign was made **visible** to passing drivers.

03 My son is considered an ordinary student.

04 Most of her work was left undone.

05 The girl at the party was found attractive.

06 Using cell phones while driving was made illegal.

07 The task was found impossible after surveying the situation.

08 She should be allowed to express her views without fear.

09 I was made to define the term 'popular culture'.

10 He was seen describing the man he saw at the crime scene.

7-4 by가 없거나 덩어리로 나오는 수동태

* She was surprised **at his bold reaction**.
* His children ware taken care **of by** his aunt.

01 The table **was covered with** dust.

02 His new album **was released** last week.

03 This masterpiece is known to the local merchants.

04 The region is known for its waterfall.

05 He is known as a fair judge.

06 My village was crowded with some scientists looking for antiques.

07 The human body is made up of many muscles.

08 Her shirt is made of silk. It looks gorgeous.

09 Butter is made from milk.

10 Her shelves were filled with fine wines.

11 Some floors are made of recycled glass and plastic.

12 By whom was this room decorated?

13 By what was the fire caused?

14 He was laughed at by his co-workers.

15 She was taken care of by her relative.

16 This old chair was got rid of by Mike.

17 I was really angry at being made fun of by my friends.

18 I was brought up by my grandparents in a big city.

19 My little brother was run over by a motor bike.

20 She was spoken ill of by her relatives.

21 He is looked up to by all of his students.

Practice A

❖ 다음 보기의 동사를 문장에 맞게 알맞게 변형해서 채우세요.

> cause   damage   find   hold   include   invite   make   show   write

01 Many accidents _____ by drunk drivers.

02 Wine _____ from grapes.

03 The neon sign _____ in a storm a few days ago.

04 You don't have to leave a trip. Service charge _____ in the bill.

05 You _____ to the wedding. Why didn't you go?

06 A movie theater is a place where movie _____

07 In Korea, elections for President _____ every five years.

08 The sign _____ in Spanish, so I couldn't understand it.

09 My wallet _____ in the parking lot at the mall.

❖ 수동태를 사용해서 문장의 뜻에 따라 의문문으로 만드세요.

01 Ask about the telephone (when / invent) : When was the telephone invented?

02 Ask about bread (how / make) :

03 Ask about the planet Mars (when / discover) :

04 Ask about copper (what / use for) :

05 Ask about the car (where / park) :

확실하게 알고 가기! some / any

a. some

정확한 숫자나 양이 표시되지 않은 경우의 수나 물건, 또는 어떤 것의 양을 의미한다.

I have **some** money to give you. [긍정문에서 큰 의미 없이 사용]

Do you want **some** milk? [권유하거나 제안하는 경우에, 유우를 좀 원해?]

Some of them don't like you. [그들 중 일부는 널 좋아하지 않아]

Some guy called for you while you were gone. [어떤 아이가 전화했다 네가 없는 동안에]

[좀, 약간, 어떤, 어느 정도]

01 We need **some apples** for this recipe.

02 Some people believe in life after death.

03 They're looking for someone with some experience.

04 I've only spent some of the money.

05 Some say it was an accident, but I don't believe it.

06 We're out of milk. Could you bring some home from the store?

07 Many of the exhibits were damaged in the fire, and some were totally destroyed.

08 Some of us realized what happened to Mike.

b. any

주로 부정문, 질문에 많이 사용되며, 긍정문에서는 강조하는 경우에 많이 사용되며,
부정, 질문에서는 일반적으로는 어느, 어떤 의 의미를 가지나 해석을 하지 않아도 되는 경우도 있다.

Do you need **any further questions**?

You can come here **any tim**e you want.

Any child who breaks the rules will be punished.

[어느, 어떤]

01 I don't have **any friends** around here.

02 Are there **any mail** for me while I was out?

03 All the stores were closed, so we couldn't buy any food.

04 This medicine didn't have any effect.

05 If I can help in any way, let me know.

06 I don't have any cash on me now.

07 Any food would be better than nothing at all.

08 Any of you should be able to answer this question.

Chapter 8 분사

* 현재 분사, 과거분사가 형용사로 사용되어 명사를 꾸며주는 형태로
현재분사는 능동으로 ~하는, 과거 분사는 수동으로 ~된으로 해석

8-1. 분사가 명사 앞에 나오는 경우

a **dancing** boy

a **broken** bowl

8-2. 지각동사

I saw the man **working** for me.

She found her bike **stolen**.

8-3. 분사가 명사 뒤에 나오는 경우

the girl **singing** on the stage

the man **invited** to the party

Practice. A. B

8-4. 감정을 나타내는 분사

a **boring** person

a **bored** person

Practice. A. B

8-1 명사를 앞에서 꾸며 주는 분사는 형용사

* The **crying** baby is looking for her mom. [우는 아이]
* Everyone stared at the **laughing** man. [웃는 남자]
* We tried to fix the **broken** bike. [고장 난 자전거]

01 The **sleeping** baby had a wet diaper.

02 The doctor fixed my **broken** bone.

03 A singing bird is outside my window.

04 You need to develop a communicating skill.

05 That rotating fan can dry all your sweat.

06 Loved people are happy people.

07 A laughing man is stronger than a suffering man.

08 I turned in my completed paper to my professor.

09 Tonight we will perform our recently finished song for you.

10 We were looking at the breathtaking scenery of the Alps.

11 I heard some inspiring words from my English teacher.

12 Rolling stones gather no moss. (속담)

13 Sarah gave a moving speech at the wedding reception.

14 She was looking at the torn letter.

15 I don't know what to do with the ruined cake.

16 His brother got a jaw-dropping gift from his girlfriend.

17 We all want to hear some encouraging words from our parents.

18 Good eating habits are the best way of preventing infection.

19 The government should do something for reduced population.

20 A watched pot never boils. (속담)

21 I prefer a pleasant-looking woman to a pretty woman.

8-2 지각동사 [see, watch, feel, hear, notice, find...]

> *We saw her **shooting** an arrow.
> *Mike heard his name **called**.

01 I heard your father **talking** with someone about a new job.

02 I felt the building **filled** up with smoke after a huge explosion.

03 We found his teacher praising Mike for his courage.

04 If I catch you stealing my apples again, there'll be trouble!

05 Officers observed him driving at 90 miles per hour.

06 We watched the sun sinking behind the coconut palms.

07 They felt a giant bear approaching them.

08 John found his leather wallet pick-pocked at the market.

09 We noticed the dog barking at the postman.

10 He observed his daughter filling out the application form.

11 I saw the child left alone crying.

8-3 형용사인 분사가 명사 뒤에 오는 경우

* We found **a man shouting** at the children. [아이들에게 소리치는 한 남자]
  [who was]

* **The table delivered** this morning is in the kitchen. [오늘 아침에 배달 된 식탁]
  [which was]

01 He brought the box **containing** food for the homeless.

02 It was costly to get a book **published** in early 1900s.

03 We shouldn't use any products polluting air.

04 This is the technology combined beauty and elegancy.

05 A beautiful girl wearing a white dress announced the results.

06 The boy performing at the concert hall now looks nervous.

07 The man found alive in the cave looks very healthy.

08 The meeting held this morning lasted more than two hours.

09 The house located on the hill will be sold at a high price.

10 The book advertised in this magazine was written by unknown author.

11 The hotel recommended by my mother provides a shoe-cleaning service for guests.

12 The average age of men exercising every day is 35 years old.

13 This is the story heard about an ancient Greek legend.

14 She took care of the passenger injured in the accident.

15 She does many curious things attracting others' attention.

16 The man explaining what happened to his family was about to cry.

17 I am looking for the boy wearing the traditional Indian clothes.

18 The cavities found among his teeth needed immediate treatment.

19 The money given to him for prize is going to be donated to a charity.

20 The man known as the captain of the spaceship used to be a war hero.

21 The decision made during the meeting will be effective immediately.

22 The boy kidnapped by his neighbor came home safe.

23 The man pleased with her quick response left her a huge tip.

24 This is the material used to make a quality jacket.

25 I think the boy looking familiar to me used to be one of my students.

26 The restaurant crowded with tourists is famous for its local dishes.

27 She entered the room, breathing deeply.

28 The urgent news reported by him was on a newspaper.

29 The victims found in the terrible earthquake needed a shelter.

30 There are still a lot of people suffering from starvation.

31 The boy compared to my son looked very angry.

32 The money left on the table will be spent for the homeless.

8-4 감정을 나타내는 분사 [느끼는지, 느끼게 하는지]

> *I felt **shocked** at her failure.
> *I heard a **shocking** story about him.

01 **The movie** we saw last week was **boring**.

02 **He** looked **surprised** to see John standing by the front door.

03 You'll be amazed by how much money we've made.

04 They have plenty of satisfied customers with their product.

05 The questions he showed us looked really confusing.

06 The speech he gave us was really touching.

07 John was getting irritated by all her questions.

08 It's amazing how much work you can do in a day if you put your mind to it.

09 He sounded pleased to get the job he wanted.

10 I felt embarrassed about how dirty my socks were.

11 Frustrated parents were calling the school to complain.

Practice A

❖ **Choose the right answer.**

01 She looks (disappointing, disappointed).

02 I found it (interesting, interested) to learn how to use tools.

03 She looked (depressing, depressed).

04 I'm sorry to keep you (waiting, waited).

05 She had her house (painting, painted) green.

06 I saw her (sleeping, to sleep, slept) in my bed.

07 She had her necklace (stealing, stolen).

08 He heard his name (calling, called).

09 I left the door (locking, locked).

10 She found her house (flooding, flooded).

11 The city (calling, called, to be called) Dallas is far from here.

12 The money (spending, spent, to spend) here is not my money.

13 It was (surprising, surprised) news.

14 I heard water (dripping, dripped).

15 I had to have this book (copying, copied).

❖ Complete the sentences using the given words.

01 The child (sleep) there is Joan.

02 The letter (write) in French is on the desk.

03 He sat (surround) by his enemies.

04 (Speak) language and (write) language are two aspects of language.

05 An (injure) man asked for help.

06 Once there lived a man (name) Kevin.

07 I felt someone (touch) my back.

08 I had my watch (repair).

09 He went away (satisfy).

10 Look at that (run) boy.

11 The gold ring (find) in the class was mine.

12 She found a letter (hide) under the table.

13 They took a walk over the (fall) leaves.

14 They sat (talk) for a long time.

15 He seemed (depress) at the news.

Chapter 9 명사절, 형용사절

9-1. 명사절 [명사가 나오는 자리에 주어+동사가 나오는 문장 형식]

A. that이 나오는 명사절

It is certain **that** he will pass the test.

B. if, whether가 나오는 명사절

I wonder **if** she is a teacher.

Practice A

9-2. 형용사절 (관계대명사)

A. 주격 [who, that, which 다음에 동사가 나와 앞에 명사를 꾸며 주는 형식]

She knows the boy **who** broke the window.

Practice A

B. 목적격 [who(m), that, which 다음에 주어+동사가 나와 앞에 명사를 꾸며 주는 형식]

I know the boy **who** you like.

Practice A, B

C. what [자체가 명사라 앞에 명사가 올 수 없고 뜻은 ~것]

What is important is your safety.

Practice A

D. whose [앞에 나온 명사의 소유격을 대신해서 사용]

She is the girl **whose** father is a judge.

Practice A

9-1 명사절 [that, if, whether]

A. that [명사가 나올 자리에 주어+동사가 나오며 이끄는 접속사는 that]

> * **That she passed the test** is true. (~것은)
>   = It is true that she passed the test.
> * The fact is **that** she got her purse stolen. (보어: ~것이다)
> * I think **that** she has a money problem. (목적어: ~다고, 라는 것을)
> * She heard the news **that** we would moved to Paris. (동격: ~라는)

01 **That she wants to be a vet** is true. (주어 위치)

02 **It** is true **that she wants to be a vet.** (가주어)

03 It's certain that he doesn't want to discuss his health matter.

04 It's pity that this wonderful time won't last.

05 It is a wonderful that she survived the disaster.

06 It was obvious that the mirror was made in India.

07 It was shocking that the swimmer drowned in the river.

08 It is unbelievable that she has improved her skill a lot in a short period of time.

09 It is really amazing that several buildings in the town have survived from medieval times.

10 It is too bad that I can't allow you to quit your job.

11 It is understandable that climate change will mean big changes for animals around the world.

12 The fact is **that she has already made several mistakes.** (보어 위치)

13 The problem is that we can't afford to buy this house.

14 The truth is that she didn't practice enough for the contest.

15 Jenny's excuse for being late was that she forgot to set her alarm.

16 Our idea is that we should move out of this house right now.

17 She thinks **that your dog looks awesome.** (목적어 위치)

18 The teacher found that the map was lying on the floor.

19 He didn't even have courtesy to say that he couldn't come.

20 We all know that a dragon is an imaginary animal.

21 Her rough hands show how hard she has worked for her family.

22 I heard that they received hundreds of job applications last year.

23 She told me that the voyage from England to India used to take 6 months.

24 We can predict that no one knows the origins of the universe.

25 The pharmacist insisted that the prescription should be correct.

26 We didn't realize that his goal was to establish a new research centre in the North.

27 Don't deny the fact **that we all are under pressure to look good.** (동격)

28 I like the idea that they can save money by buying quality products.

29 The fact that he is your friend should not affect your decision.

30 There's no question that Susie recognized the difficulty of the problem.

31 The fact that every detail of my trip is so clear in my mind makes me happy.

32 The root cause of cyber violence is the fact that Internet users are not communicating.

B. if, whether: [~인지] 나오는 명사절, 그리고 관용적인 용법 [~인 것처럼 보인다]

> *I don't know **if** she is honest.
> *He asked me **whether** I wanted to play tennis this afternoon.
> ***It seems that** everyone has completed their homework. [It은 가주어처럼 의미 없이 필요에 의해 사용]

01 I wonder **if** his cell phone has many functions just like mine.

02 I doubt **whether** she can describe how he looks in detail.

03 He is not sure if she has measured the height of the ceiling.

04 I will find out if he has any previous experience with this type of work.

05 I will ask her whether she is interested in physics or chemistry.

06 We are not sure if he could struggle to overcome his shyness.

07 Whether or not we will go to the beach this weekend depends on the weather.

08 **It seems that** she did nothing wrong to them. [관용적인 용법]

09 **It is likely that** our candidate is going to win in the election.

10 It does not seem that body weight is a good predictor of running speed.

11 It seems likely that they will release the hostages soon.

Practice A

❖ **다음 중 빈 칸에 알맞은 것을 고르시오.**

01 She wants to find out (that / if) Mike is still in America.

02 He and I believe (that / if) you will join the club.

03 The problem is (that / weather) we don't have enough time.

04 We will check (that / if) all the customers arrived on time.

05 It is certain (that / if) David will pass the test.

06 I'm not sure (that / if) this chance is good for us or not.

07 I will ask Mike (that / if) he can give me some money.

08 Nobody thinks (that / if) our teacher will give us the homework.

09 I don't know (that / if) Jenny can win the game or not.

10 We wonder (that / if) the weather will be fine tomorrow.

11 My teacher was sure (that / if) his students were honest.

12 I do not doubt (that / if) they will keep the promise with me.

13 Peter knows (that / if) we are not in trouble.

14 I can't believe (that / if) John made a big mistake.

15 I told him (that / if) I could solve the problems.

9-2 형용사절은 관계대명사

A 주격 관계대명사: 앞에 나온 명사를 꾸며 주는 형용사 역할의 동사

* An elephant is **an anima**l that (which) **lives in hot countries.**
  동물 ← 사는 더운 나라에

* **Children** who **hate chocolate** are uncommon.
  아이들은 ← 싫어하는

01 I know a boy **who** likes you.

02 John works at a factory **that** makes all kinds of umbrellas.

03 You will need a coat **which** will keep you warm.

04 Marie Curie is the woman who discovered radium.

05 I have a rich friend who tries to lead a normal life.

06 This is the girl who has a deep male voice.

07 There will be a festival that will attract huge crowds.

08 There were spectators who screamed with delight.

09 He is not a person who will betray us.

10 You should encourage the children who have failed the test.

11 Mike is the boy who never expresses his emotions to us.

12 I will invite the woman who supported me during the election.

13 There are many insects that lay countless eggs at a time.

14 Mike is the person who can quickly notice some change in her.

15 She knows a man who often talks about his trip to the North Pole.

16 We wanted explanation from the men who disagreed to our plan.

17 I'm the one who feels more anxious about my future.

18 I'm looking for a friend who has a lot in common with me.

19 This is the company that makes quality furniture.

20 I visited the country which used to be a colony of French.

21 I want to marry someone who has a high level of mental ability.

22 We are willing to find shelters for people who lost their houses in the fire.

23 She is the lady who spent her whole life helping disabled people.

24 We need to find someone who can donate $1,000 to cancer research.

25 We often see many athletes who like to enjoy their moment of glory.

26 Those who need more space can use my basement. (중요: 일반 사람들로 해석)

27 The boy who maintains high grades studies 3 hours every day.

28 The house that has three rooms and a huge garage will be sold soon.

29 The boy who likes to enjoy a new adventure will be your roommate.

30 The girl who dyed her hair pink likes wearing colorful clothes.

31 The museum which holds many sculptures will have an exhibition next week.

32 The wallet that was found in the laboratory is in my desk drawer.

33 A teacher who seldom gives students praise and encouragement neglects his duty.

34 The water that flows into our area from Japan is still not safe to drink.

35 The man who robbed the old lady ran away but was arrested next day.

36 The only country that has been divided into two parts in the world is Korea.

37 Women who have long hair may believe it makes them more appealing.

38 Chemicals which are harmful to children shouldn't be used at all.

39 The man who organized charity has worked for our community for a long time.

40 The girl who often tells me a lie about her parents thinks I am stupid enough to believe her.

Practice A

❖ 다음 괄호 안에서 알맞은 것을 고르시오.

01 I know the boy (who / which) ate your cake.

02 I yelled at the puppy (who / which) was biting my shoes.

03 I have a friend (who / which) is good at swimming.

04 She often makes a cake (which / who) tastes good.

05 This is the house (who / which) has a pretty garden.

06 I know the cook (who / which) comes from America.

07 I really hate a man (who / which) smokes in a public place.

08 Mr. Kim is the driver (who / which) always drives carefully.

09 She likes to read a book which (has / have) many interesting drawings.

10 The boy who looks healthy (do / does) exercise every day.

11 The man who sent me the flowers (work / works) at a bank.

12 The girl who (like / likes) me really (speaks / speak) English well.

13 I invited a few people who (work / works) with me.

14 The girl who is singing on the stage (is / are) my daughter.

15 The volunteer who (help / helps) us usually comes here on Sunday.

9-2 형용사절은 관계대명사

B 목적격 : 앞에 나온 명사를 꾸며 주는 형용사 역할의 주어+동사

* Bring the tool **which we were using last week.**
  도구　　　← 　우리가 사용했던 지난주에

* The doctor **who(m) I saw was very friendly.**
  의사　　　← 　내가 보았던

01 She likes the boy **whom** I like.

02 This is the girl **who** I want to meet today.

03 You can take all the eggs **that** I gathered this morning.

04 I don't like the gift that he sent me on my wedding anniversary.

05 She is wearing a yellow shirt that I bought her last week.

06 This is the ruins which most people have never been to.

07 I can't afford to go on the trip which you have planned for us.

08 She has the evidence that we were all looking for.

09 Most stars don't have the private life that everyone enjoys.

10 She has a lifestyle which most people would envy.

11 Many of the children will encounter some difficulty which they haven't expected.

12 Cabbage and lettuce are vegetables which we usually enjoy in our daily life.

13 You gave me a word of encouragement which I will never forget.

14 This is the man whom most athletes like to compete with.

15 This is the motion which you should repeat over and over for your back.

16 I can repeat all the sentences which you wrote on the board.

17 You can't have everything that you desire.

18 Jenny often neglects the duties which she is supposed to do.

19 I will take care of the problem that we can't afford to ignore.

20 My son can discover the physical characteristics of objects which most kids can't.

21 The life span of whales which everyone knows is wrong.

22 I need some glue which I can use to put these pieces of furniture together.

23 The laptop which I use for work is lightweight.

24 Sadly, the blind man who you will treat today will slowly go deaf.

25 The boy who I met today was independent and ambitious.

26 The city which you can explore today has rural landscape and many skyscrapers.

27 Sorry, but the idea that he suggested to us was worthless.

28 The man who you introduced to me has a strong sense of justice.

29 The flowers which she planted last year are going to bloom beautifully.

30 The apples that they planted were ruined by the storms.

31 The crop that they harvested will be exported all over the world.

32 Fear that you feel when you fly is nothing serious.

33 The novel which I read on vacation was a page-turner.

34 Community problems which we discuss every month are different case by case.

35 The restaurant which they recommended turned out to be great.

36 The participants who I interviewed met me at the local library.

37 The results that I obtained may bring positive social change.

38 The puppy that your giant dog bit needs a serious medical treatment.

39 The house which he occupies without paying the rent is not his uncle's.

40 The city **in which** I was born has a beautiful scenery. [전치사 + 관계대명사]

41 This is the job from which you can get valuable experience.

42 I need to find someone with whom I can cross the border.

43 The company at which I work treats its employees well.

44 The store at which we bought the furniture offered a discount.

45 The hometown in which he grew up has developed into a big city.

46 The boy to whom I taught English has improved a lot.

47 The house in which we used to live was recently renovated.

48 I will find a man from whom you can get some professional opinions.

49 The experiment **(which)** they conducted yielded interesting results. [생략]

50 The surprise party he arranged last week was a disaster.

51 The disasters we experience every year are floods and droughts.

52 The fur coat she is wearing looks very luxurious.

53 The assignment my teacher gave me is too difficult to finish in a day.

54 You don't know the noise you make makes people irritated.

55 The freedom we enjoy now resulted from efforts of our ancestors.

56 The painting you are looking at will be sold at a high price.

57 Modern life we enjoy now resulted from some scientists' efforts.

58 The man I brought here led a movement to stop destruction of the rain forest.

59 The Galaxy is the large group of stars which our sun and its planets belong to.

60 This is **something** that I inherited from my father. (것)

61 Mike is **someone** that you can talk to about your money problem. (사람)

62 **The only** person that I can depend on is my father. (유일한)

63 **All** that I need today is some cash to buy food. (단지)

64 All we need to do right now is **take** a rest.

65 He is **the very** man that she would marry next month. (바로 그)

Practice A

❖ 다음 빈 칸에 알맞은 것을 고르시오. (답이 두 개 될 수도 있음)

01 She wants to meet a person (who / whom) she can depend on.

02 He will invite someone (who / whom) can give us a speech.

03 Mike wants to have the watch (that / which) I bought at the mall.

04 We can use the pen (which / that) I put on the table.

05 John will bring the children (who / whom) I have to take care of.

06 Did you talked with the ladies (who / whom) want to go to the party?

07 I'm going to watch the movie (that / which) he borrowed from his friend.

08 This is the car (that / which) my father drives to work every day.

09 This is the woman (who / whom) always wants to try something new.

10 The boy whom you are going to teach English (study / studies) really hard.

11 The people whom she works with at the museum (has / have) a good sense of humor.

12 We would like to introduce to you the man (who / whom) you all want to meet.

13 Mike is the boy (who / whom) I'd like to introduce to you.

Chapter 9 명사절, 형용사절

Practice B

❖ 다음 중 어법상 어색한 부분을 바르게 고쳐 쓰시오.

01 This is not a common mistake that anyone can make it.

02 I know the woman whom wants to talk with you.

03 He will sell the car that his father has driven it for a long time.

04 Mike knows the boy whom often takes away my books.

05 The cell phone which I bought for my father work very well.

06 This is the man whom can protect us from the enemy.

07 I have to clean the room which you messed it up.

08 The boy who I often teach him math is doing well at school.

09 The TV program which I watch every day often make me laugh.

10 The school she will build for students are in a good location.

11 The book that she read it was important for her history review.

12 The girl that I walk to school drops by at 8 am.

13 This is the house I lived when I first came to the United States.

14 This is the news article which I have been looking for it.

15 Let's go to a country which the sun always shines.

9-2 형용사절은 관계대명사

C what : 자체가 명사라 앞에 명사가 나올 수 없으며 [~것] 으로 해석

* **What she has** is not hers   [주어]
* This is **what she fixed**.   [보어]
* I gave her **what he needed**.   [목적어]

01 **What she didn't consider** was his emotion. [주어]

02 What he is anxious about is his father's health.

03 What I did was separate students into four groups.

04 What is not effective is our educational system.

05 What they need right now is harmony between them.

06 What is necessary for them now is food and shelter.

07 What you have just seen is human nature.

08 What that child needs are care and affection.

09 What distinguishes them from us is a color of skin.

10 What is precious is her sacrifice for the poor.

11 What he hates is to live in a greedy and selfish society.

12 This bracelet is **what** I got from my father. [보어]

13 It is not what she experimented on animals.

14 I am what matters here, not you.

15 Calling names is what caused Mike to get into a fight.

16 This is what we can do in a very short period of time.

17 She will limit **what** we can do here. [목적어]

18 I am proud of what you have done for them.

19 Some people are honest enough to return what isn't theirs.

20 Some people don't consider what they shouldn't do in a public area.

21 She will donate what she has earned while working here last year.

22 People tend to see only what they really need.

23 Use what you know about yourself to find the most effective way to study.

Practice A

❖ **다음 빈 칸을 완성 한 후에 해석을 쓰시오. (what, that)**

01 She gave me (what) she had kept for a long time.
⇨ 그녀는 그녀가 오랫동안 가지고 있었던 것을 나에게 주었다.

02 He gave me everything (   ) he had owned for a long time.
⇨ _____

03 She gave me something (   ) I wanted to have.
⇨ _____

04 (   ) she has is not mine.
⇨ _____

05 (   ) she is a nurse is not true.
⇨ _____

06 The problem is (   ) we are running out of time.
⇨ _____

07 The problem is (   ) we have is not good enough.
⇨ _____

08 I'm interested in (   ) you have just told me.
⇨ _____

09 This is (   ) she brought to me yesterday.
⇨ _____

10 The fact is (   ) she forgot (   ) she needed.
⇨ _____

❖ 다음 빈 칸을 완성 한 후에 해석을 쓰시오. (what, that)

11 She believes _____ her sister is old enough to drive.

⇨ _____

12 He believes _____ she did was right for all of us.

⇨ _____

13 _____ made her make him leave was his tight schedule.

⇨ _____

14 The idea _____ John told us about the trip was amazing.

⇨ _____

15 The idea _____ she wants to build her house by the lake is not good.

⇨ _____

16 I'd like to know _____ you know about me.

⇨ _____

17 I'd like to know _____ you came here on time.

⇨ _____

18 It is true _____ she gave up studying in England.

⇨ _____

19 _____ is important is she is from England.

⇨ _____

9-2 형용사절은 관계대명사

D whose : 앞에 나온 명사의 소유격 [~을 소유한, 가진, ~의: 사람, 사물 둘 다 적용]

* I know a boy. **His** father is a judge.
* I know a boy **whose** father is a judge.
  판사인 아빠가 있는

01 I met a woman **whose son** is an astronaut.

02 Jenny always wears a skirt **whose design** I don't like.

03 She is the pianist whose performance gets a lot of attention.

04 They make fun of the man whose name sounds funny.

05 She hired an agent whose job is simple and clear.

06 The woman whose hair is long enough to touch the ground is a pharmacist.

07 She's the scientist whose research has been internationally recognized.

08 This is a city whose purpose is to maximize the opportunities for all member of society.

09 A person whose name and face everyone knows is called a celebrity.

10 The artist whose work is displayed at the museum is a local talent.

Practice A

❖ 다음 빈칸에 알맞은 것을 고르시오.

01 She likes to have a friend (who, whose) hobby is the same as hers.

02 He chose the plate (which, of which) the color is green.

03 I work with a woman (who, whose) goes to school after work.

04 Mike knows some people (who, whose) job is getting rid of insects.

05 She wants to buy a TV (which, whose) screen is the widest of all.

06 Sam is the boy (who, whose) sister won the speech contest.

07 The doctor (who, whose) patients suffer Alzheimer's treats no other patients.

08 Peter knows the woman (who, whose) son has the same problem as his son.

09 He carefully opened the door (which, whose) windows were broken.

10 You can look up the word (which, whose) meaning you don't know.

11 Mike wants to talk with a girl (who, whose) rides a motor bike.

12 She has a friend (who, whose) look is like a monkey.

Chapter 10 전치사

명사, 대명사, 동명사 앞에 사용되는 단어 또는 단어 군으로 방향, 시간, 장소, 위치, 공간적 관계를 나타내거나 대상을 소개하는 데 사용된다.

1. 명사 앞에 위치
2. 문장 속 단어 간의 관계를 설명한다.
3. 방향, 시간, 공간, 위치 등을 나타낸다.

a. 시간

a	시간	on	요일 / 날짜
in	달 / 년도 / 계절	until	까지
for	~ 동안	from	~로 부터

b. 장소 / 방향

to	~로 (도착지)	at	~에 (지점)
in	~안에서 혹은 ~에서	on	~위에
under	아래에	below	아래에
over	위에 (표면과 닿지 않은)	behind	~뒤에
around	주위에	through	~을 통과하여
across	~을 가로질러	along	~을 따라서
toward	~ 쪽으로, 향하여	out of	~로부터(벗어나)
above	~위에	opposite	반대편에

c. 수단, 도구, 소유, 기타

by	~에 의해, (시간) ~쯤	in	~으로 (언어, 방식)
of	~의 (소유)	into	~안으로 (동작)
about	~에 관해, 대략	against	~에 반대하여
like	~처럼	on	~에 대해, ~에 관해
with	~을 가지고, ~와 함께	onto	~위로 (동작)

10-1 전치사 [명사, 대명사, 동명사 앞에 위치]

* The man **in** black looks scary.
  검은 옷에 남자

* Zen is the title **of** the movie.
  영화의 제목

* There is violence **against** elderly people.
  노인들에 대한

01 She left here **at** a quarter after ten. [전치사는 명사 다음에 해석]

02 I decided to write a poem **about** my mother's life.

03 I'm **against** all forms of hunting.

04 They show no respect **for** their boss.

05 Many rich people own the paintings of Picasso.

06 Don't show this letter to anyone else.

07 She wrote her name in capital letters.

08 He was wearing a green shirt with yellow stripes.

09 We are still waiting for the main dish.

10 I'm trying to have a healthy diet in a healthy way.

11 Don't write anything below this line.

12 We can see the spaceship fly over our heads tomorrow.

13 I didn't mention his name during the meeting.

14 She came from the opposite direction.

15 He walked through the door and took the broom.

16 There are a lot of rats in grain fields.

17 The policeman behind us will put her in jail.

18 My teacher gave a touching speech to us.

19 She is the ideal and perfect person for the job.

20 A man with a gun came into the restaurant.

21 The water came above our knees.

22 No one my age collects stamps as a hobby.

23 She shouted my name in a sharp voice.

24 We walked along the river for quite a long time.

25 This area of the country is mostly desert.

26 I met a girl with a long dark curly hair.

27 More people are choosing to work beyond retirement age.

28 I don't feel ashamed of myself.

29 Children's pictures decorated the walls of the classroom.

30 Mark is always behind the rest of his class in math.

31 Fill this jar with cold water now.

32 I spent a few days in a small island during holidays.

33 He has a bruise just above his left eye.

34 We all know him as a news reporter.

35 This insect lays its eggs on a dead leaf.

36 His uncle died of cancer last week.

37 She got carsick and had to get out of the car for some fresh air.

38 Computers are an essential part of modern life.

39 This is a perfect cage for an animal like a hippo.

40 She lost her sight in accident and became blind last year.

41 He has to go to school for the deaf.

42 Your tie matches well with your suit.

43 He noticed two policemen coming towards him.

44 Cabbage is not a usual food for American.

45 We all go on a picnic except Mike.

46 You are here as my guest, so feel comfortable.

47 He uses his elbow instead of his finger to press the button.

48 One of the world's oldest cars is on display in Seoul today.

49 Lamb is the meat of a young sheep.

50 A spider is not a kind of bug. It is kind of animal.

51 The chief reason for cavities is sweets.

52 I can't really tell you anything beyond what you know already.

❖ 주요 전치사 뜻 쓰기

01 Most of us _____

02 in pencil _____

03 in a mild voice _____

04 any books on India _____

05 about his age _____

06 about 10 miles away _____

07 around the village _____

08 the road to London _____

09 someone like you _____

10 from Seoul to Spain _____

11 by the window _____

12 over the world _____

13 over the fence _____

14 below the line _____

15 above the roof _____

16 someone behind me _____

17 beyond the village _____

18 against the wall _____

Chapter 11 대명사

11-1. 부정대명사 [특정한 대상을 가리키지 않는 대명사]

one, the other, another, the others

Take this **one**, and I will take **the other**.
John will meet this lady, and I will meet **the others**.
If you don't like this one, you can have **another**.

11-2. 재귀대명사 [강조인가, 목적어인가]

myself, herself, himself, ourselves, themselves...

I can do it **myself**.
You should love **yourself**.

11-1 대명사 [one, the other, others, the others, another]

> * one: 앞에 나온 같은 종류의 명사를 가리키는 경우나 일반적인 사람을 가리키는 경우
> * one, the other: 대상이 둘 있는 경우: 하나, 다른 하나
> * another: 같은 종류 중에서 또 다른 하나
> * one, the others: 하나, 나머지
> * some, others: 어떤, 또 어떤

01 I have a camera at home. Do you have **one**, too?

02 I like all the pictures except this **one**.

03 I have a few books on Korean food. You can borrow **one** if you want.

04 **One** should take good care of himself.

05 One should make the effort to vote.

06 Mike took this road, but John took **the other**.

07 Here's **one** sock, but where's the other one?

08 You can park on **the other** side of the street.

09 There will be **another** bus along in a few minutes.

10 I chose this jacket after all because **the other ones** were all too expensive.

11 Some people believe in life after death, others don't.

12 Buy two pairs of underwear and get another pair completely free.

13 He passed away **the other day** at the age of 904. [최근에, 언젠가]

14 She's much brighter than all the other children in her class.

15 There are one or two other problems I'd like to discuss.

16 I think we need another two hours to complete the task.

17 To say is **one** thing, to do is quite **another**. [A와 B는 별개의 것이다]

18 We hitch-hiked home in the storm, and another two hours went by before we finally made it back.

19 She has five different kinds of pets. One is a cat, another is a turtle, the others are puppies.

20 It's one thing to say we have a goal; it's another to actually act on it.

11-2 재귀대명사 [목적어: ~자신을 / 강조: 스스로]

* You should blame **yourself** for what happened. [목적어]
* If you want something done right, you'd better do it **yourself**. [강조]

01 I take good care of **myself** all the time. [생략 불가]

02 Why do I always have to do everything **myself**? [생략 가능]

03 His name is James but he calls himself Jim.

04 It was the boss himself who opened the door.

05 We have to ask ourselves if we can help them.

06 They have to do something to protect themselves.

07 Why don't they just do it themselves?

08 The dog was looking at itself in the mirror.

09 I think the problem is the car itself.

10 Heaven helps those who help themselves. [those:는 사람들로 해석: 격언]

Chapter 12 접속사 [두 문장을 연결하며, 일반적으로 접속사 다음에 주어+동사가 나옵니다.]

12-1. 양보 [비록 ~일지라도]

Although S + V

Even though

Though

Even if [가정: 설사 ~일지라도]

While [~인 반면에, ~일지라도]

Despite [~에도 불구하고] + 명사 혹은 동명사

In spite of

Although she is busy, she never neglects anything.
Despite being careful, she made a few mistake.

12-2. 상관

Both A and B	[A와 B 둘 다]
Either A or B	[A 혹은 B 중에 하나]
Neither A nor B	[A도 아니고 B도 아니고]
Not only A but [also] B	[A뿐만 아니라 B도]
Not A but B	[A가 아니라 B]

12-1 양보 [though, although, even though, *despite, in spite of]

* **Even though** it was cold, we went for a walk.
  비록 추웠을지라도, 우리는 산책을 나갔다.

* **While** this dress is really good, it's still expensive.
  이 드레스가 정말로 좋을 지라도, 그것은 여전히 비싸다.

01 I like him though he makes me angry sometimes.

02 Although he makes good money, he never wastes any.

03 Even though he's 20 now, he's still like a little child.

04 Though Malta is a very small island, its history is long and rich.

05 Although the car's old, it still runs well.

06 I still look fat, even though I've been exercising regularly.

07 Everything I told them was correct, though I forgot a few things.

08 They will probably win, though no one else thinks so.

09 Even though she hasn't really got the time, she still offers to help.

10 I don't usually drink coffee. I've had 2 cups today though. (however)

11 **Even if** I fail the test, I won't try it again. [설사 ~일지라도]

12 He's going to buy the farm even if they raise the price.

13 Even if he gets accepted to Harvard, he won't be able to afford the tuition.

14 One person wants out, **while** the other wants the relationship to continue. [~인 반면에, 일지라도]

15 While there was no clear evidence, most people thought he was guilty.

16 While she is a likable girl, she can be extremely difficult to work with.

17 We played soccer **in spite of** the rain. [~에도 불구하고]

18 He won despite the fact that he was injured.

19 They fell in love in spite of the language barrier.

20 She went to Spain despite the fact that her doctor had told her to rest.

21 Despite all our efforts to save the factory, the boss decided to close it.

12-2 상관 [둘 이상의 단어가 함께 쓰여야 하는 접속사]

[Both A and B, either A or B, neither A nor B, not only, but also]

* **Both** she **and** I agree to the plan. [A와 B 둘 다]
* You can stay **either** with me **or** with Janet. [A 혹은 B 둘 중에 하나]
* **Neither** Brian **nor** his wife mentioned anything about moving house. [A도 아니고 B도 아니고]
* She is **not only** intelligent **but [also]** humble. [A뿐만 아니라 B도]
* This is **not** her ring **but** mine. [A가 아니라 B]

01 She can **both** speak **and** write Japanese.

02 Both he and his wife work at the same company.

03 Cathy will not have both cake and ice cream.

04 **Either** mom **or** dad will come to pick you up.

05 You need to speak a foreign language, either Spanish or French.

06 An estimated 3.5 billion people either watch or play football.

07 This vehicle can use either natural gas or a conventional fuel.

08 Either I drive to the airport or I get a taxi.

09 I have never been to either England or France.

10 *****Either** of the candidates **is** good. [대명사]

11 I will **neither** call you **nor** send you a message before midday.

12 The equipment is neither accurate nor safe.

13 Neither Mike nor John can financially support you any more.

14 Neither Brian nor his wife mentioned anything about moving to another house.

15 ***Neither** of them was interested in going to university. [대명사]

16 My father is **not only** a writer **but also** an actor. [also 생략 가능]

17 Not only Mike but also John received some cash from my uncle.

18 The nurses want not only a pay increase, but also reduced working hours.

19 Simplicity of language is not only powerful, but perhaps even respectable.

20 It's **not** me **but** Tim who messed everything up

21 I see you're in the mood not for desserts but appetizers.

Chapter 13 가정법

13-1. 가정법 과거: 현재 사실의 반대되는 상황을 표현할 때 사용

If 주어 + 과거 동사, 주어 + would, could, might + 동사원형
I wish + 주어 + 과거동사

Practice A

13-2. 가정법 과거 완료: 과거 사실의 반대되는 상황을 표현할 때 사용

If 주어 + had p. p, 주어 + would, could, might + have p. p
I wish + 주어 + had p. p

Practice B

13-1 가정법 과거 [If 주어 + 과거 동사, 주어 + would, could, might + 동사원형]

> * If she **were** here, I **would** be happy.
>   만약에 그녀가 여기 있다면, 나는 행복할 텐데.
>
> * I wish I **had** a son like you.
>   내가 너와 같은 아들이 있다면 좋을 텐데.

01 If you **were** in my shoes, what **would** you do?

02 If he **knew** where I am, he **would keep** in touch with me.

03 If I didn't apologize, I'd feel guilty.

04 If I invited her to the party, it would be a disaster.

05 If I inherited a billion dollars, I would travel to the moon.

06 If I owned a zoo, I might let people interact with the animals more.

07 If she admitted that it is her fault, he would forgive her.

08 Everyone would be unhappy if the flight were delayed.

09 I wish she **could see** how much her actions affect the other students.

10 I wish he visited us more often. I feel lonely when he is not around.

11 I wish it weren't so hot these days. It is hard to make it hard to sleep.

12 I wish I were not distracted by the sound of a car alarm in the street.

13-2 가정법 과거완료 [If 주어 + had p. p, 주어 + would, could, might + have p. p]

> * If I **had been** at the party. I **could have met** him.
>   만약에 내가 파티에 갔었더라면, 나는 그를 만날 수 있었을 텐데..
>
> * I wish I **had seen** that movie.
>   내가 그 영화를 봤다면 좋았을 텐데.

01 If you **had told** me you needed a ride, I **would have left** earlier.

02 If I **had cleaned** the house, I **could have gone** to the movies.

03 If it had rained, we would have gotten wet.

04 If I had had more money, I could have bought new furniture.

05 If I had accepted his offer, I would have made good money.

06 If he had consumed enough nutrition, he would have been healthy.

07 If she had raised awareness of a love of nature, we could have get more fund.

08 If they had had more time, the project would have been completed within budget.

09 If the severe drought hadn't caused most of the crop to fail. they wouldn't have suffered from starvation.

10 I wish he had done what he had neglected to do.

11 I wish I **hadn't made** the same mistake I had made before.

12 I wish he hadn't ignored my warning signals.

Practice A

❖ 괄호 안의 동사를 알맞은 형태로 바꿔 쓰시오.

01 If he _____ a little harder, he _____ pass the exam. (study, can)

02 If I _____ his phone number, I _____ call him right now. (know, will)

03 If she _____ money, she _____ buy something to eat. (have, can)

04 If you _____ in my place, what _____ you do first? (be, will)

05 If she _____ me, I _____ finish the work early. (help, can)

06 If he _____ a mistake, he _____ get that job. (make, will)

07 If you _____ exercise, you _____ be healthy. (do, will)

08 If they _____ to our plan, we _____ take a trip tomorrow. (agree, can)

09 If she _____ her mind, he _____ accept her suggestion. (change, will)

10 If he _____ there, I _____ feel happy. (go, will)

11 내가 춤을 잘 추면 좋을 텐데. (be) = I wish I _____ good at dancing.

12 내가 너를 도와줄 수 있다면 좋을 텐데. (can) = I wish I _____ help you.

13 컴퓨터가 있으면 좋을 텐데. (have) = I wish I _____ a computer.

14 내가 유명 영화배우라면 좋을 텐데. (be) = I wish I _____ a famous movie star.

15 내가 시험에 통과한다면 좋을 텐데. (can) = I wish I _____ pass the exam.

Practice B

❖ ❖ 다음 주어진 동사를 이용하여 빈 칸을 완성하시오.

01 If she _____ his condition, she _____ him. (know, help)
    만약 그녀가 그의 상태를 알았더라면, 그녀는 그를 도와주었을 텐데.

02 If it _____, I _____ more than two. (be, buy)
    만약 그것이 쌌더라면, 나는 그것을 두 개 이상 샀을 텐데.

03 If he _____ my advice, he _____ in what he did. (accept, succeed)
    만약 그가 나의 충고를 받아들였더라면, 그는 그가 하는 것에 성공했을 텐데.

04 If they _____ dinner before they left, they _____ the train (have, miss)
    만약 그들이 떠나기 전에 저녁을 먹었더라면, 그들은 기차를 놓쳤을 텐데.

05 If we _____ money, we _____ a new house. (waste, buy)
    만약 우리가 돈을 낭비하지 않았더라면, 우리는 새 집을 살 수 있었을 텐데.

06 If you _____ the weather, we _____ more time. (check, save)
    만약 당신이 날씨를 확인 했더라면, 우리는 시간을 더 절약 할 수 있었는데.

07 If she _____ him, she _____ happy. (marry, be)
    만약 그녀가 그와 결혼을 했더라면, 그녀는 행복했을 텐데.

08 If he _____ enough time, he _____ it today. (have, complete)
    만약 그가 충분한 시간이 있었더라면, 그는 그것을 오늘 완성했을 텐데.

09 I wish I _____ him yesterday. (meet)
    내가 어제 그를 만났더라면 좋았을 텐데.

10 I wish I _____. (move out) I miss the old place.
    내가 이사를 가지 않았더라면 좋았을 텐데.

11 I wish I _____ there yesterday. (go) I really had to meet him.
    내가 어제 그곳에 갔었더라면 좋았을 텐데.

12 I wish I _____ money. (have) I had to buy that bike yesterday.
    내가 돈이 있었더라면 좋았을 텐데.

memo